More Joy of Photography

More Joy of Photography

The Editors of Eastman Kodak Company

Addison-Wesley Publishing Company

More Joy of Photography Staff

Eastman Kodak Company

Keith A. Boas	Author and Editorial Coordinator
John I. Fish	Managing Editor
Robert E. Brink	Production Supervisor
Elizabeth J. Riedman	Production
Charles W. Styles	Production
Annette L. Dufek	Production
Norman C. Kerr	Equipment Photography
William Paris	Photo Research
Deborah Connor	Editorial
Michelle D. Crawforth	Editorial
Judith L. Johnston	Editorial

Addison-Wesley Publishing Company

Doe Coover	Editor
Paul Souza	Designer, WGBH Design
Jim Georgeu	Vice President of Manufacturing
Donald F. Earnest	Text Editor
Hubert C. Birnbaum	Technical Text Editor
Lynn Gaertner	Copy Editor
Donald M. Chaffee	Indexer
Lorraine Ferguson	Production Assistant
Gaye Korbet	Production Assistant
ZeeAnn MacDonald	Production Assistant
Stephanie Fleischer	Technical Illustrator

Cover photograph still life by Norman Kerr
Cover photographs, top to bottom:
Neil Montanus
Keith Boas
Michael Newler
Keith Boas
Neil Montanus
© 1981 Bill Carter

Copyright © 1981 by Eastman Kodak Company
Philippines copyright © 1981 by Eastman Kodak Company

ISBN 0-201-04544-3
ISBN 0-201-04543-5 paperback

ABCDEFGHIJ-KR-854321

Library of Congress Cataloging in Publication Data
Main entry under title:
More joy of photography.
 Continues: The joy of photography.
 Includes index.
 1. Photography. I. Eastman Kodak Company.
TR146.M626   770   81-10776
ISBN 0-201-04544-3   AACR2
ISBN 0-201-04543-5 (pbk.)

First printing, August 1981

More Joy of Photography
was set in the Zapf International family of typefaces by DEKR Corporation of Woburn, Massachusetts.

The design and production were supplied by WGBH Design, Boston, Massachusetts.

The color separations and camera work were supplied by Rochester Prep, Inc., of Rochester, New York.

W. A. Krueger Company of New Berlin, Wisconsin, printed and bound the book on 70-pound Warrenflo stock from Lindenmeyr Paper Company.

Contents

Frank Phillips

Introduction

Part I

The Creative Process

Charles R. Vines

Part II

Creative Controls

Keith Boas

Part III

100 Techniques for More Creative Photographs

Special Situations

Special
Techniques

Special
Equipment

Special
Effects

Introduction

The world of creative photography is an adventuresome one in which the photographer's vision prevails. Drawing from a wide array of tools and techniques, the creative photographer picks and chooses those that will best convey an idea on film. Sometimes this means altering or distorting reality through the use of special filters or lenses; at other times it means reducing the elements of a scene to an abstract composition; at still other times it can mean letting a representational image speak for itself. As a creative photographer, your challenge is twofold: you need to perceive a subject in your own way, and you need to be able to execute your interpretation of it technically.

More Joy of Photography is designed to help you with both aspects of this challenge. Through pictures and text, we hope to inspire you aesthetically as well as instruct you technically. Although this book is a sequel to *The Joy of Photography*, you do not need to know everything in that book to enjoy this one or to find it useful. A working knowledge of cameras will be helpful, but even that isn't necessary, since we review the basics of camera handling in Part II. If you have read *The Joy of Photography*, you'll probably recognize some of the same topics here; the process of good picture taking is an ongoing one that requires constant practice. In this book we've expanded these topics with new ideas as well as more detailed technical information. We've also organized the book so it will be easy to use.

In Part I, **The Creative Process,** we discuss the ways you can develop a personal style of photography by becoming better attuned to the photographic possibilities in the world around you. A special section called ***In Focus*** features six very different professional photographers – Pete Turner, Elliott Erwitt, Ernst Haas, Duane Michals, Jan Groover, and Harry Callahan – who show their pictures and discuss their own personal approaches to photography.

Part II, **Creative Controls,** presents the technical information you need to know to use your equipment for better results. After a brief review of camera basics, we discuss the visual variables of a scene – motion, perspective, and light – and show how you can effectively manipulate them to achieve the effect you want.

Part III, ***100 Techniques for More Creative Photographs,*** is the heart of the book. Here you'll find more than 200 pages of specific ways that you can make your photographs more exciting and original. In four sections – Special Situations, Special Techniques, Special Equipment, and Special Effects – you'll learn how to see pictures in new places, from everyday still lifes to color abstractions; how and when to break the rules; how to adapt your camera to unusual photographic conditions such as fireworks, moonlight, and mirror reflections; how to perform creative techniques such as blurring and panning; how to use filters, lenses, and flash more creatively; and how to manipulate both your camera and the environment for a host of special effects, from multiple exposures and trick scale to blacklight photography and panoramas. All of the techniques presented can be done with your camera and its basic accessories or with a processed slide or print. There is no special darkroom work involved.

A motion-picture director once said that a good technique is successful when the audience isn't really aware of it. Technique should not be an obvious result but rather a gentle means to that end. As a photographer, you are more than a button pusher; you can strive for photographs that reflect your soul, not ones that are merely clinical examples of technique. It is our hope that you use the techniques presented in *More Joy of Photography* in this way – as stepping stones to your own visual expression. Be individual in your picture taking and enjoy the personal rewards.

Introduction

The world of creative photography is an adventuresome one in which the photographer's vision prevails. Drawing from a wide array of tools and techniques, the creative photographer picks and chooses those that will best convey an idea on film. Sometimes this means altering or distorting reality through the use of special filters or lenses; at other times it means reducing the elements of a scene to an abstract composition; at still other times it can mean letting a representational image speak for itself. As a creative photographer, your challenge is twofold: you need to perceive a subject in your own way, and you need to be able to execute your interpretation of it technically.

More Joy of Photography is designed to help you with both aspects of this challenge. Through pictures and text, we hope to inspire you aesthetically as well as instruct you technically. Although this book is a sequel to *The Joy of Photography*, you do not need to know everything in that book to enjoy this one or to find it useful. A working knowledge of cameras will be helpful, but even that isn't necessary, since we review the basics of camera handling in Part II. If you have read *The Joy of Photography*, you'll probably recognize some of the same topics here; the process of good picture taking is an ongoing one that requires constant practice. In this book we've expanded these topics with new ideas as well as more detailed technical information. We've also organized the book so it will be easy to use.

In Part I, **The Creative Process,** we discuss the ways you can develop a personal style of photography by becoming better attuned to the photographic possibilities in the world around you. A special section called **In Focus** features six very different professional photographers – Pete Turner, Elliott Erwitt, Ernst Haas, Duane Michals, Jan Groover, and Harry Callahan – who show their pictures and discuss their own personal approaches to photography.

Part II, **Creative Controls,** presents the technical information you need to know to use your equipment for better results. After a brief review of camera basics, we discuss the visual variables of a scene – motion, perspective, and light – and show how you can effectively manipulate them to achieve the effect you want.

Part III, **100 Techniques for More Creative Photographs,** is the heart of the book. Here you'll find more than 200 pages of specific ways that you can make your photographs more exciting and original. In four sections – Special Situations, Special Techniques, Special Equipment, and Special Effects – you'll learn how to see pictures in new places, from everyday still lifes to color abstractions; how and when to break the rules; how to adapt your camera to unusual photographic conditions such as fireworks, moonlight, and mirror reflections; how to perform creative techniques such as blurring and panning; how to use filters, lenses, and flash more creatively; and how to manipulate both your camera and the environment for a host of special effects, from multiple exposures and trick scale to blacklight photography and panoramas. All of the techniques presented can be done with your camera and its basic accessories or with a processed slide or print. There is no special darkroom work involved.

A motion-picture director once said that a good technique is successful when the audience isn't really aware of it. Technique should not be an obvious result but rather a gentle means to that end. As a photographer, you are more than a button pusher; you can strive for photographs that reflect your soul, not ones that are merely clinical examples of technique. It is our hope that you use the techniques presented in *More Joy of Photography* in this way – as stepping stones to your own visual expression. Be individual in your picture taking and enjoy the personal rewards.

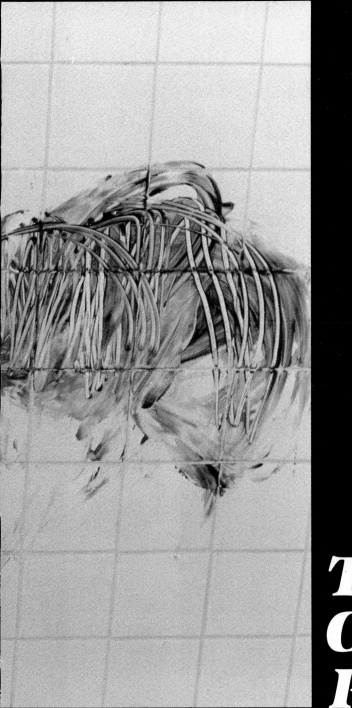

The Creative Process

From Science to Art

"Photography as a fad is well-nigh on its last legs, thanks principally to the bicycle craze." Famous photographer Alfred Stieglitz proclaimed this demise of photography in 1917. As the hand-held camera had captured the public's fancy a few years earlier, so now would the bicycle, he felt, and thousands would forsake Sunday snapshooting strolls for riding upon the newfangled contraption.

Nothing could have been further from the truth. In the ensuing decades, photography has permeated every part of life, as an instrument of both science and enjoyment, and an influence on other art forms and our perceptions of the world. With the camera and its related forms, television and cinema, the farthest peoples become neighbors, and seemingly remote events come to bear on us instantly, intimately.

Yet photography as most of us know it, as a hobby or vocation, is a private endeavor. We make personal statements with our photographs, whether we realize it or not. The subjects we choose and the techniques we employ to capture these subjects say a great deal about who we are.

Photography has the power to do more than reproduce what we see, however. It can transform the particular to the universal, the mundane to the poetic. And it is when we add our personal vision to the technology of photography that we cross that line from mere reproduction to transformation. With this shift from science to art, we begin speaking with a vocabulary of aesthetics, not just a vocabulary of

technology. With this shift we enter the world of creative photography.

You will not find any set rules for becoming a creative photographer. It is important to have command of the technical skills required for photography, of course, and Part II of this book will review those basics and reinforce their importance. But these skills are essentially simple ones, and, once learned and practiced, they will become virtually automatic. More importantly, these skills can serve as the basis of experimentation and exploration, allowing you the freedom to express yourself in new, more creative ways.

In the pages that follow, we will look at some of the ideas that professional photographers have about personal style and creativity. Then in Part III, you will find 100 different techniques for more creative photographs. We hope all of this information will serve to spark new ideas for your own pictures, because that is what *More Joy of Photography* is all about.

Russell Lamb

Pierre Stea

Photographers have often captured the simple joy of a mother-child embrace. Yet here the message is fresh and expressive.

James Dieffenwierth

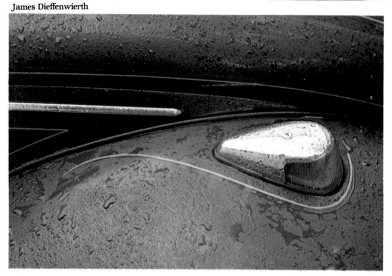

A tight close-up of a gleaming car fender is a surprisingly delicate study in line, shape, and color.

Sequoia National Park at dawn offers a sweeping vista that sums up the majesty and grandeur of nature.

Practicing for Spontaneity

Like all creative arts, photography requires practice. The concert pianist works daily on finger exercises, the ballet artist attends classes throughout his or her career. As a photographer, you need your own special kind of practice.

First, it's important to practice seeing good pictures. You need to sharpen your senses to the world around you, begin to notice small details, motion, colors, shadows. A creative photographer is a spontaneous one, one who can see picture-taking possibilities in ordinary situations that other people might miss, such as noticing how the leaves in a grape arbor create a mirror pattern on the ground below. Master photographer Minor White referred to the special readiness required for photography as a blank state of mind, "a very receptive state of mind, . . . not unlike a sheet of film itself – seemingly inert, yet so sensitive that a fraction of a second's exposure conceives a life in it."

Second, photographers need practice in the skills required to respond quickly to a good picture. You need to sharpen your reflexes until the basic camera controls – setting the aperture and shutter speed, focusing, and releasing the shutter – become second nature to you. If you must deliberate for more than a fraction of a second over them, many a good picture will be lost.

Finally, you should practice being spontaneous. While this might seem a contradiction in terms, you can achieve it by allowing yourself to react naturally to the subjects that move you. Learn to let a subject speak to you – and learn to listen. Think about how you can use the right technique and equipment to say something different, something personal, with your picture.

A good way to practice all three of these elements is to give yourself assignments, such as taking pictures of a grove of woods, or photographing the meaning of friendship, or expressing what you think about the city. Spend some time on your assignments. Think about them, walk around your subjects, try different equipment and techniques. Then spread your pictures out on the floor or project them. What do they say about your personal vision?

Not every photograph needs to be a masterpiece. Nor will it be. Any professional photographer will tell you that in a roll of thirty-six exposures you'll be lucky to find one or two that seem right. Photographer Harry Callahan says he often shoots ten rolls of film to pick just three pictures that he likes. The process of becoming a good photographer is a continuing one.

Jeanette Gheeraert

Being spontaneous means having a camera handy when a scene like this presents itself.

Colorfully stockinged feet, seen from an unusual angle and without their owners, create an exuberant, playful scene.

One hardly notices the figure in this scene, as she is as bespeckled by the leaves' shadows as the ground is. A wide-angle lens (see page 172) accentuates the foreground canopy, imparting a feeling of movement to the scene.

Simplicity Is the Goal

R. A. Armstrong

Good technique is often confused with gimmickry or with a showy display of equipment. Many beginning photographers mistakenly think that a lot of lenses, filters, and expensive accessories will make them better photographers overnight, that a colored filter or distorting lens is all it takes to turn an ordinary snapshot into a work of art. Sometimes these devices are appropriate, and throughout Part III you will see exciting photographs for which they have been used. But most serious photographers would agree that simplicity – in technique, in equipment, and in vision – is a far more effective photographic tool.

"Ultimately, simplicity is the goal – in every art," commercial photographer Pete Turner says, "and achieving simplicity is one of the hardest things to do. Yet it's easily the most essential." As cameras become more sophisticated, the tendency to use more elaborate techniques and equipment is strong. Yet for beginners, especially, less equipment is usually better. Pete Turner suggests you start with your camera and one lens, either a wide-angle or a telephoto, and work with that and a specific subject. Black-and-white artist Duane Michals agrees, and admits to being suspicious of people who make a big display of equipment. Having a minimum of equipment allows you to remain in control of the situation and of your photograph, and it allows you to concentrate on what is really important – how your photograph should look.

Simplicity in vision is also important. You don't have to go around the world to take good photographs. Master photographer Imogen Cunningham is well known for her sensuous black-and-white pictures of calla lilies and various other exotic flowers and plants. In fact, she took almost all of these pictures in her backyard garden at home. Ernst Haas, who does travel extensively for his photographs, still notes, "To be very strong with the simplest subject, the most banal situation, is to be really creative." Harry Callahan agrees: "The photographs that excite me are photographs that say something in a new manner; not for the sake of being different, but ones that are different because the individual is different and the individual expresses himself."

Simplicity can also mean being selective, focusing in closely on a subject, isolating it from a distracting or unessential background, as Edward Weston did in the photograph of shells here. You should strive for simplicity in choosing subject matter. Look for strong shapes and lines and distinct patterns.

Often the most striking photographs are those that make a single, stark statement, such as the photograph above. By crouching low and photographing the child with a telephoto lens, the photographer was able to convey effectively her hopeless, frightened feelings. It's a picture that literally pulls your heartstrings.

The poignancy of this portrait of a child is heightened by the photographer's choice of camera angle and time of day. Picturing her from a low angle removed any foreground distractions, and the golden light of late afternoon added a sympathetic touch of warmth.

Dana Brown

Laura Embry

Edward Weston

By stepping back to take a long view of England's Windsor Castle, the photographer has also captured the elegant symmetry of the imposing building and its grounds.

It took no special equipment to capture the essence of a garden stroll, just a quick and observant eye. By focusing in close on her subjects, the photographer emphasized the many floral images in the scene, from the ladies' dresses to the real flowers in the foreground.

A close view and an overhead angle allow the intricate, graceful forms of shells on a rocky beach to come to the fore in this photograph by Edward Weston.

Challenging Assumptions

Great philosophers have long pondered the nature of creativity. It is the one human impulse all arts and sciences have in common; it is the quality that links bold thinkers of all fields, from the Wright brothers to Albert Einstein to Ernest Hemingway.

One major characteristic of creative art is that it challenges assumptions of the visual world around us. Picasso saw figures as irregularly arranged cubist shapes; Van Gogh's wheat fields and skies were pulsating dabs of pigment. These techniques, like your photographic techniques, conveyed what the artists felt about their subjects.

Photography is the ideal medium in which to challenge assumptions, because of all art forms, it is the one people most expect to represent reality. Duane Michals says photographers have a wonderful weapon they too seldom take advantage of: people believe photographers and thus bring to them a set of expectations. The creative photographer grapples with these expectations, shaping or altering reality by the way he or she approaches a subject.

For example, we expect a photograph of a tower to display its height, or a photograph of a leaf to highlight its curving shape. Yet by choosing an unorthodox angle of view, the photographers of the pictures here were able to offer fresh insights into the subjects, to challenge the standard, predictable ways we perceive them.

Photographer Aaron Siskind's advice sums it up: "We look at the world and see what we have learned to believe is there. We have been conditioned to expect. . . . But, as photographers, we must learn to relax our beliefs. Move on objects with your eye straight on, to the left, around on the right. Watch them grow large as you approach, group and regroup as you shift your position. Relationships gradually emerge and sometimes assert themselves with finality. And that's your picture."

O. J. Roth

Viewed from underneath, a worm-ravaged leaf becomes an almost abstract study in subtle shades of green.

Dr. George Gill

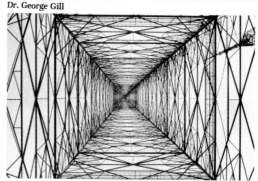

Looking straight up also gives this photographer an unusual- and unexpected- perspective of a radio tower, reducing it to a composition of lines.

Norman Kerr

Colour Library International

Using a variation of a technique called panning (see page 158), this photographer effectively conveys the swaying motion of a hammock, while providing a colorful, dynamic image.

Conventional composition rules would dictate that this racer be placed closer to the center of the image. But by capturing him as though he were about to race off the edge of the picture, the photographer offers us a startling interpretation of the peril of the sport.

Making Connections

Photographs can also challenge our assumptions of the world by making unexpected connections. A creative photographer can bring together seemingly unrelated ideas, objects, or events in a way that leads to a new conception. It can be seeing a chair propped against a door as the touch of a nonchalant decorator. It can also be taking a perfectly normal situation – like a painter at work on a billboard – and seeing the humor in the accidental connection of a man in running clothes painting . . . a man in running clothes.

Making connections implies that you see things in new ways, imparting your personal vision to the interpretation of a subject. It means looking at the ordinary with a childlike curiosity and wonder, transforming the familiar to the strange and the strange to the familiar. Making connections creates order out of the chaos that the objective world presents to your eye. When you transfer a subject from its visual context to a piece of film, your personal experience is the link, the connection, that determines everything – how that subject will look, how others will perceive it, and what message it ultimately offers about you.

Finally, you must learn to make connections in your work. As a photographer, you will discover that certain subjects, spatial relationships, and color balances continue to show up in your pictures. The techniques become easier to achieve, the results become more pleasing. This is a major step in the art of creative photography, when the translation from seeing to doing is automatic, when the camera has "lured you, then compelled you," as Minor White has said, "to create through seeing."

On the other side of the photograph, the viewer makes his or her own connections. Five different people can look at the same photograph and come away with five different interpretations of it. Part of the power of photography is the unique alliance between photographer and viewer created by pictures. Each party brings a set of attitudes, thoughts, and experiences to a picture, and the good photographer recognizes the connection he is capable of making. "I believe strongly in photography," Harry Callahan says, "and hope by following it intuitively that when the photographs are looked at they will touch the spirit in people."

Glenn Stillwell

Seeing humor in everyday life can produce some intriguing images with stories to tell. Spontaneity and a good eye are the keys.

A splash of spilled paint and a chair propping open a door in this muted still life tell us the occupants have probably been redecorating recently.

When photographing people, think about posing them with the tools of their trade. This man's ladle hints of his profession – a chef in a restaurant in China.

Learn to look for patterns in scenes. In this window full of pineapples in a Fiji market, notice how both color and line contribute to the overall effect.

Finding Inspiration

As a creative photographer, you must allow yourself to be moved by what you see and feel. You must also seek stimulation from other sources. What inspires creative photographers? Most would agree, first, that photography does! The process of taking pictures and seeing the results is a continually fulfilling one. But beyond that, the photographers interviewed for the *In Focus* portfolios agree that all photographers – young and old, aspiring and professional – should seek inspiration from other art forms and media, not just from photographers and photographs.

While many photographers admit to being influenced by the work of such greats as Henri Cartier-Bresson or Paul Strand, some think that too conscious a study of other photographers' work can produce imitation, not originality. Duane Michals believes that too many photographers are "so constipated visually that they don't have the energy to see things their own way." The solution, he says, is to stop looking at photographs for awhile, "to unlearn, which is much harder than learning, to develop the strength of your own convictions, to trust your own taste, your own judgment."

Elliott Erwitt and Ernst Haas both cite music and other art forms as inspiration photographers should seek out. "If you try to be inspired by a great poet or a great piece of music, you're not going to copy anyone," Haas says. "You're going to find yourself much faster through something you can't copy directly."

Haas tells of being a young boy in Austria during the German occupation. Every night families gathered in secrecy to listen to the BBC broadcast for news of Allied progress. The broadcast always opened with the first four notes of Beethoven's Fifth Symphony – *da da da dum.* "It was a very important symbol," he recalls, for the BBC was the region's only source of non-propaganda news. As a photographer in Vienna after the war, Haas found that he was constantly taking pictures of three items in a row and a fourth lower than the first three: three standing lampposts and a fourth one bent over from a bomb, three birds perched on a fence and a fourth flying down and away. Suddenly he realized he was unconsciously photographing *da da da dum.*

Susan Conroy

A graphic image such as this one is usually set up by the photographer for its impact and design qualities.

► A slow shutter speed used to capture a moving subject results in a blurry picture. Yet here the deliberate use of the technique creates an enigmatic portrait of a pianist at work.

Rick Opiola

When you begin photographing it's inevitable that you will imitate other photographers, unconsciously or consciously. But allowing yourself to react and respond personally requires taking risks. Taking risks means being daring, trying new methods, new solutions, and new ideas without control over the outcome. To do so, you can't be afraid of being wrong. If you try an unusual photographic technique for the first time, chances are you'll see some less than wonderful results in the beginning. But only by taking the risk initially will you ultimately produce the photograph that no one else could. Only by taking risks will you learn to go beyond imitation to creativity and your own personal style of photography.

14

Developing a Personal Style

Too often we skim the world around us, taking in only a fraction of the shapes, surfaces, colors, and events that are present. Scenes and people you see every day can present you with new, fresh images and exciting photographic possibilities if you take time to examine your thoughts and feelings about them, analyze their visual attributes, and consider the various ways of arranging and presenting those elements.

As a creative photographer, you must ultimately learn to trust your eye and to follow your instincts, to develop a sense of personal taste. Your eye – and the link it symbolizes between your brain and your emotions – is what can help you shape that taste. By broadening your visual horizons you will learn to see better pictures. One way of doing this is simply to look around more, to be more conscious of your environment and its visual attributes. Another way, suggested by each of the photographers featured in the interviews that follow, is to pay attention to all of the visual arts – painting, sculpture, drawing, and architecture, as well as photography. From them you can develop a sense of overall art appreciation that will help you to identify what attracts you visually so you can duplicate it on film.

As we have seen, it is also important to experiment with photography, to try the unknown and test your skills. By stretching the limits of your picture taking you will develop a better sense of your aesthetic preferences, of your own personal style. This style will most likely evolve and change as you do, for the creative photographer uses pictures as vehicles for expressing his or her personality, perceptions, and preferences. As both an art form and a method of communication, then, photography has infinite possibilities. "We must remember that a photograph can hold just as much as we put into it," Ansel Adams has said, "and no one has ever approached the full possibilities of the medium."

In the pages that follow we will look at the work of six accomplished photographers with distinct yet different personal styles, and for each we display a picture that the photographer has chosen as representative of his or her work. While these pictures vary a great deal, the photographers' messages – and their love of photography – are surprisingly similar.

Ernst Haas

The warm tranquility of a lake at sunset is presented in this richly colored composition.

Ernst Haas's evocative portrait of a barefoot Mexican boy expresses his unchildlike burden and isolation.

In Focus: Pete Turner

Pete Turner is perhaps best known for his commercial photography, an amazing array of images that are seen in magazines and books and on billboards, posters, and record album jackets. Many of these images, ranging from bathroom fixtures to spaceships, border on the surreal. "A photographer's work is given shape and style by his personal vision," Turner explains. "It is not simply technique but the way he looks at life and the world around him. I have always been a science fiction reader, and I think this comes through in my work."

But Pete Turner's work has another side, a private side. "I usually follow what I call parallel lines in work. One is my commercial work to earn a living, and the other is my fine art work, which I do to please myself. One fertilizes the other."

Whatever the motivation of his photography, Pete Turner works with deliberation and planning. He usually has a goal in mind when he photographs, and he frequently researches the subject and the area where he plans to shoot. For the photo here, he knew he wanted to photograph the mysterious monuments at Stonehenge with a full moon as backdrop, so he checked the astronomical charts and planned his visit to England accordingly.

But Turner is not above altering or manipulating the environment. "I do *make* pictures," he allows. He frequently rearranges a scene or creates one out of scattered elements. For his famous picture of cannonballs, he relates how he found the pile and moved it around to form the image he wanted. "Being ready for the unexpected is part of the fun of photography, but I think it helps to have achievable goals if you're going out to shoot. Have a subject in mind, even if it's as general as a beach or trees, and work with that," he suggests. "A lot of times, in trying to achieve that linear goal of, say, photographing trees, the person very well might come upon something totally unexpected."

Pete Turner has been photographing since the sixth grade, when he owned a Brownie camera. Encouraged by his family, he knew at a young age what he wanted to do, and he later attended the Rochester Institute of Technology. As one of their most illustrious alumni, he now returns to lecture.

Martha Pearson

ANTONIUS   HENDRIKUS MARIA

BoS

If the term *iconoclast* applies to any photographer featured in these pages, it is Duane Michals. His work is often the subject of controversy in the art community, a condition he accepts as a consequence of his nonconformist view of photography.

Michals's chief inspiration comes from the surrealist painters. "The surrealists always contradict people's assumptions; photographers never do," he says. "Photographers show you what a sunset looks like, they show you what a moonrise over Hernandez looks like, they show you women's breasts or empty car lots, but they don't play with your mind. . . . I'm not saying all photographers should play with your mind, but it's an option they don't exercise. I think photographs should be provocative and not tell you what you already know. It takes no great powers or magic to reproduce somebody's face in a photograph. The magic is in seeing people in new ways."

It is portraits, particularly portraits of painters such as René Magritte or Andy Warhol, that many people associate with Michals. He doesn't have a studio but prefers to photograph people in their own environments, working in black and white and using only existing light. The picture here was taken at the Stedeleijk Museum in Amsterdam. The backdrop is a piece of sculpture by Daniel Spoerri that shows a table, fully set, hanging vertically on the wall. The model is a young student Michals met in Holland. "As soon as I saw the sculpture, I knew I could do this," he recalls. "A man perpendicular to a table is contradictory to your assumptions about life."

Michals compares his photography to fiction writing. Unlike journalistic or editorial photographers, who document historical events, Michals says that his photographs are products of the imagination; his scenes would have no reality without him. "I like to place a familiar object in an unfamiliar context," he says, "to play games in photographs."

His advice to photographers is to develop their intuition. "Trust that little voice in your head that says 'Wouldn't it be interesting if . . .' And then do it. You have to have the courage to take the first step, to take that first picture. Everything else is just noise."

In Focus: # Ernst Haas

Ernst Haas is an internationally recognized
photographer who has worked in virtually
every aspect of photography – journalistic,
fine art, and commercial. He was born and
raised in Vienna, and although he resides in
New York City today, much of his work still
takes him to Europe.

The picture here was taken when
he was on assignment to photograph the
1980 Oktoberfest in Munich for a German
magazine. The festival was interrupted by a
violent terrorist bombing, and Haas relates
how the event affected his picture taking.
"Suddenly I began seeing a parallel between
the violence of the bombing and much of
the festival. The aggression and hostility of
carnival rides seemed not unlike that of the
frantic reactions I had witnessed just days
before, during the attack."

Haas is frequently moved by such
events and moods. "For me it is important to
forget myself when I photograph," he says,
"to be totally loose and react in a way that
will surprise me, too." If a photographer
loses himself in the act of photographing, he
finds himself again, Haas believes, in seeing
the results and knowing which pictures
are the good ones, which ones say what
you want and work for you. And how
does one know the good pictures from
the bad? "The best pictures differentiate
themselves by nuances," Haas maintains,
"a tiny relationship – either a harmony or a
disharmony – that creates a picture." Often
this tiny nuance is not visible at first. "I like
my pictures to look loose with a hidden
structure," he says, "to look quite banal in
the beginning but then to speak to the viewer
more and more. The longer you look at it, the
better it gets."

Ernst Haas is famous for the motion
technique he displays in the photo at left, but
he is insistent that a photographer should
develop many techniques for his repertoire.
"Photographers shouldn't have just one
technique – would you read just one book?
Have just one friend?" Ultimately, technique
must serve the larger purpose of vision. Haas
believes strongly that a good photographer
has to have enough command of technique
that, even when not inspired by a subject he
will take a good picture – and when he is
inspired, he won't lose it.

In Focus: Elliott Erwitt

"The whole point of taking pictures is so you don't have to explain things with words," says Elliott Erwitt, "so why bother with them? I care about instinctive photography."

The muses that inspire Erwitt's instinctive photographs are varied. There are dogs, of course, and the sea. And humor. An early book of dog photographs was called *Son of Bitch*; he hopes to call a collection of seaside images *Son of Beach*, or perhaps *Beside the Seaside*. When asked to what he ascribes the sense of humor that pervades much of his work, he replies, "Genes, I guess."

Erwitt began photographing in high school in Los Angeles, where his parents had emigrated from Europe. He worked as a candid photographer and in photo labs, including a stint for a firm that mass printed movie star portraits. In one week he produced 25,000 Ingrid Bergmans.

Once Erwitt had established himself in New York it didn't take long for magazine editors and advertising executives to discover his talent, and for over twenty-five years now he has remained at the top of his profession. When he does commercial work, he always carries two cameras–one for the assignment and one for his personal pictures. The photo here was taken while Erwitt was photographing a New York *Times* Magazine fashion layout on boots and shoes in Central Park. Suddenly he was inspired to crouch down and snap with his own camera.

He shoots all his personal photographs in black and white. Color, he feels, is too easy, and when something is easy, people get sloppy. With black-and-white photography, one deals with abstraction, a reduction of the elements and a more basic kind of composition. "You don't have prettiness to help you out," he says. "I've always thought a great achievement would be to take a spectacular sunset picture in black and white." A joke? Perhaps a little one.

"You can find pictures everywhere," Erwitt contends. "It's simply a matter of noticing things and organizing them. You just have to care about what's around you and have a concern with humanity and the human comedy. People who don't are interested in nothing."

25

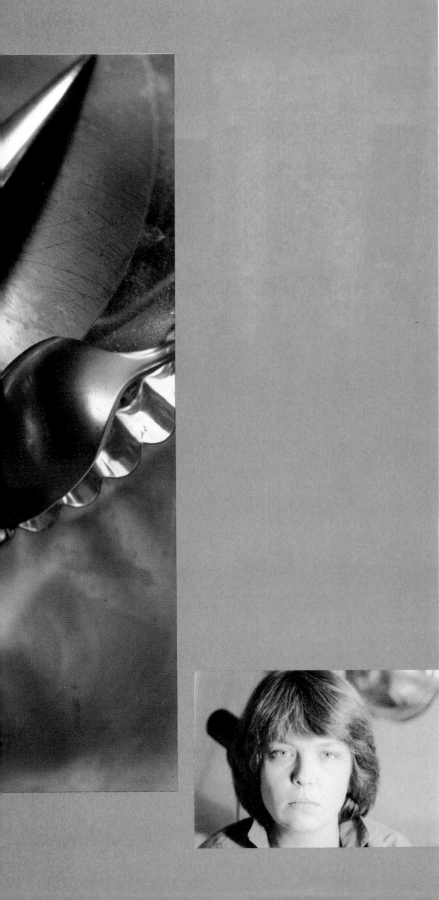

In Focus:

Jan Groover

Jan Groover bought her first camera a year after finishing a degree at Pratt Institute in New York. She had studied painting and was teaching art in public schools when she won a fellowship to study art education at Ohio State University. It was there she first began photographing in color, and it was only a short time later that she gave up her palette and brushes to devote herself to photography. "There came a moment," she says, "when I just wasn't a painter anymore."

She still speaks of photographs in painterly terms. Her work, principally still lifes of kitchen accoutrements, deals with spaces and shapes and colors. The subject matter came about almost by accident. "When I began doing still lifes I went out and bought dried flowers, vases, and yards of background cloth," she relates, "because they were the props of the most conventional still lifes, and I thought that would be an interesting place to start." But the pictures weren't pleasing to her, so she resumed other work.

Then in January 1978 the National Endowment for the Arts awarded her a grant, which enabled her to buy a 4×5 inch format view camera. She bought more dried flowers and went back to still lifes. But the 4×5 pictures were still unsatisfactory – only more so, because they were bigger.

"Out of frustration I took the camera over to the kitchen sink and began photographing. Suddenly I realized I had finally matched the tool with the vision. With the 35 mm camera, it was difficult to move in close enough to the objects for such intimate work. With the 4×5 I can move the camera as much as I move the still life for the precise kind of drawing I want."

Groover feels that good photographs should inspire an emotional response – from the photographer as well as the viewer. While it is not always possible – or desirable – to analyze that response, it is essential for the serious photographer to know as much as possible about his instincts, tastes, and aesthetic preferences. "You have to follow your nose," she says, "to have a mental attitude about what you feel good about and yearn for in a picture." The first step to that goal? "Being able to say 'I like it' or 'I don't like it.' That's first."

Harry Callahan

"I love art," says Harry Callahan, "because it doesn't have rules like baseball. The only rule is to be good. That's the toughest thing to do." Harry Callahan has been doing "the toughest thing" since 1938, when he bought his first camera, a Rolleicord. He had gone into the camera store to buy a movie camera because he admired his brother-in-law's, but the clerk convinced him a still camera would be more to his liking.

By 1941 Harry Callahan had joined the Detroit Photo Guild, a photohobbyist group, and had begun amassing a body of photographic work. He soon found himself on the faculty of Chicago's Institute of Design, and in 1946 he had his first one-man show at the 750 Studio Gallery in Chicago.

Callahan explains that he "grew up" with photography – and as new lenses, filters, and other accessories were manufactured, he enjoyed experimenting and "playing" with them. Many of his most striking images, in fact, are made with wide-angle and telephoto lenses, and he is recognized as a master of the multiple exposure.

The photograph at left is from a series done in Ireland in 1979 and is typical of his work in another dimension: color. Although Callahan had taken color photographs since the 1940s, he never showed them publicly until 1976. Now, he says, color is the medium he prefers. In some of his photographs, a single color dominates and resonates in subtle variations of the hue; in others, such as this one, a detail of color serves his purpose.

"I feel a little bit like a painter," explains Callahan. "A painter applies brush stroke after brush stroke, working toward something. It's just a matter of knowing when to quit." The photographer works similarly, he believes, taking roll after roll of film, searching for the perfect image. "You know it's in there somewhere," he states.

Photography, like life, is an adventure to Harry Callahan, and his advice to photographers is to embrace that adventure, to explore and experiment and try new things. He remembers with resentment that early teachers told him photography was a mystery and that it would take him 25 years to get where they were. "The mystery isn't in the technique," corrects Harry Callahan, "it's in each of us."

Ricker Winsor – Woodfin Camp Associates

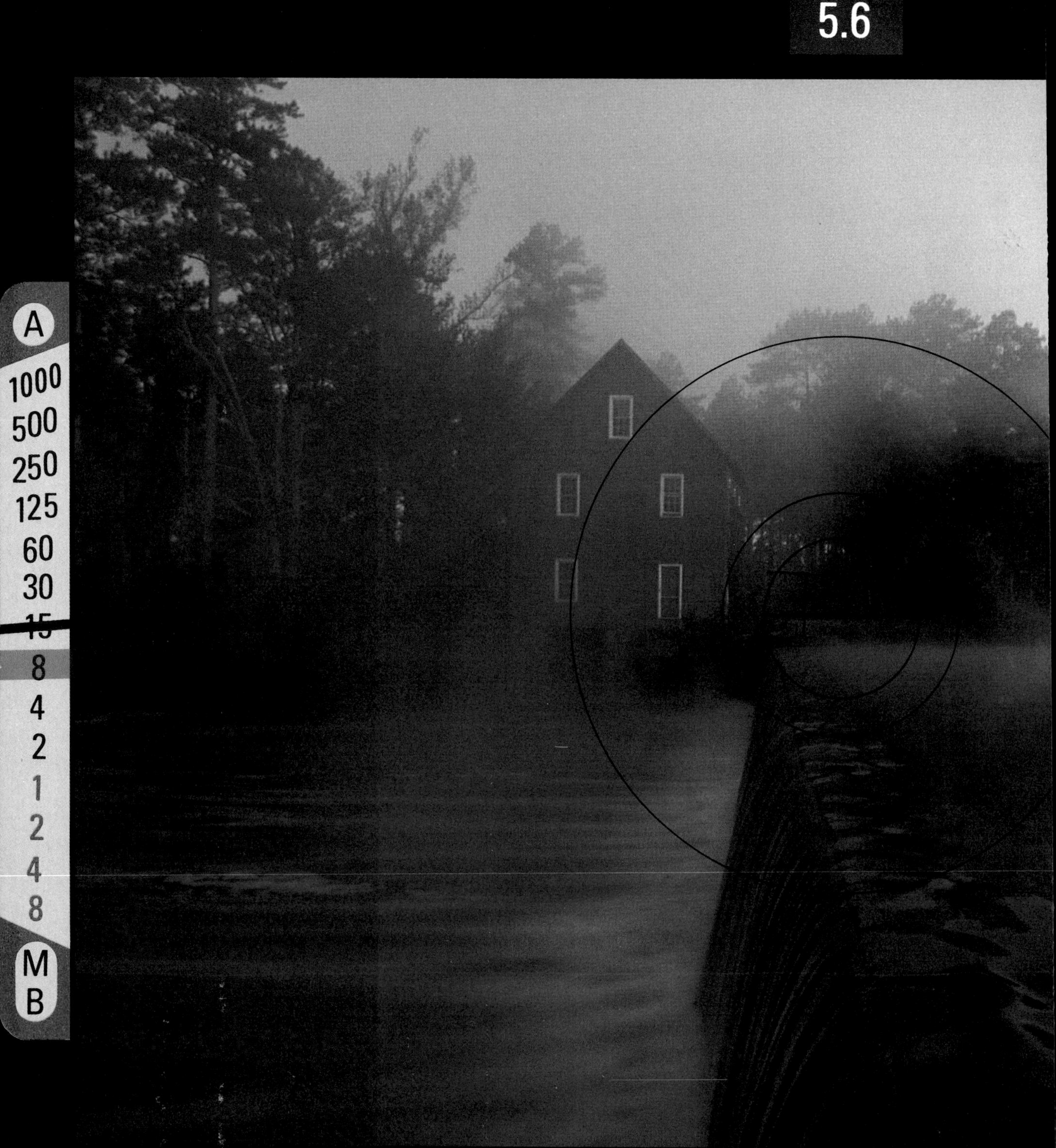
5.6
A
1000
500
250
125
60
30
15
8
4
2
1
2
4
8
M
B

Part II

Creative
Controls

The 35 mm Camera

To take successful pictures, you need a working knowledge of the basic camera features at your fingertips. But you must also understand the visual variables of your subject and interpret them for the effects you want. These variables include the subject's range of focus, its motion, the distance and angle of view from which you photograph, and the qualities of natural and artificial light that you must transfer to film. After a brief review of camera mechanics we will explore these variables.

Although a seasoned photographer will probably be able to take good pictures with any properly functioning camera, the features of various camera models can make a difference. For many photographers, 35 mm cameras present an appealing combination of features. The 35 mm film frame measures 24 × 36 mm (approximately 1 × 1-1/2 inches) – large enough to make considerable enlargements or projected images of excellent quality. At the same time, a 135-film magazine with enough film to make 36 or more exposures is small enough to fit in a compact, lightweight camera body.

Smaller film formats allow greater camera miniaturization, but the reduced film area limits satisfactory print size. In contrast, larger roll-film cameras that accept 120-size film produce bigger film frames, which in turn offer improved enlargeability. However, the larger film size of these medium-format cameras dictates a bigger, heavier camera.

Regardless of the size of the film in your camera, you have to be able to aim it accurately and focus the lens so it will form a clear, sharp image of your subject when sharpness and clarity are your aims. Hand-held cameras commonly employ either optical viewfinders or single-lens reflex viewfinders as focusing tools.

Optical viewfinders let you look at the subject through a viewing system separate from the camera lens. An etched or "floating" frame outlines the subject for composing the picture. In viewfinders that feature automatic parallax correction, the frame shifts position as you change the focus setting, to provide accurate framing over a range of distances. Some optical viewfinders also have a central coincidence rangefinder coupled to the lens. As you adjust the lens focus, the rangefinder indicates whether or not your subject will be in sharp focus.

Rangefinder cameras provide a clear, bright view of the subject, and most people find them easy to focus accurately, even in dim light. They are limited, however, in the optical accessories that can be attached for special effects.

Single-lens reflex (SLR) cameras use a movable reflex mirror in the camera body to divert light passing through the lens to a matte-surface viewing and focusing screen. When you look through the eyepiece, you focus and compose virtually the same image that will be recorded on film, no matter what lens or accessory is used. The view is less bright than that seen through a rangefinder camera's viewfinder. But many photographers happily accept the trade-off to obtain the greater versatility of the SLR. To focus an SLR, you adjust the lens until the principal subject is clearly defined on the focusing screen. The transition from blur to crisp image is gradual and sometimes difficult to judge. Many SLRs, therefore, incorporate focusing aids in their viewing screens, such as split-image and microprism fields.

Nearly all modern rangefinder and SLR cameras have built-in exposure meters coupled to lens-aperture and shutter-speed controls. Manual models require you to adjust the lens opening or shutter speed until an indicator signals a proper exposure setting. Automatic exposure cameras adjust the aperture, shutter speed, or both in response to changing light levels. These two models – and the adjustments required when you want to override your camera's system – are discussed in greater detail on page 36.

The major operating controls and features of a typical 35 mm SLR camera are illustrated and labeled in the pictures here. Not all cameras necessarily have all these features, nor do these features represent all those that may be found on a given camera. Always consult your camera's instruction manual for the specific features and how to use them on your camera. Some of the basic ones are:

Aperture ring: *adjusts the lens opening to admit more or less light and controls depth of field.*

Focusing ring: *rotates to adjust focus.*

Shutter-speed dial: *regulates the length of time film is exposed to light and controls the way moving subjects are rendered on film.*

Film-speed dial: *when set to the ISO/ASA speed of the film you're using, it tells the exposure meter how sensitive the film is to light.*

Depth-of-field preview button: *allows you to preview the image that will be projected onto the film during exposure.*

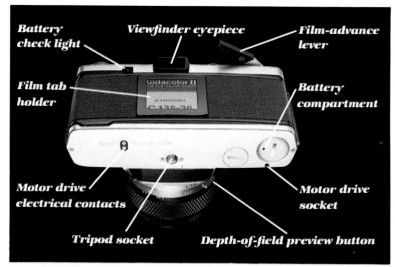

Battery check light · Viewfinder eyepiece · Film-advance lever · Film tab holder · Battery compartment · Motor drive electrical contacts · Tripod socket · Depth-of-field preview button · Motor drive socket

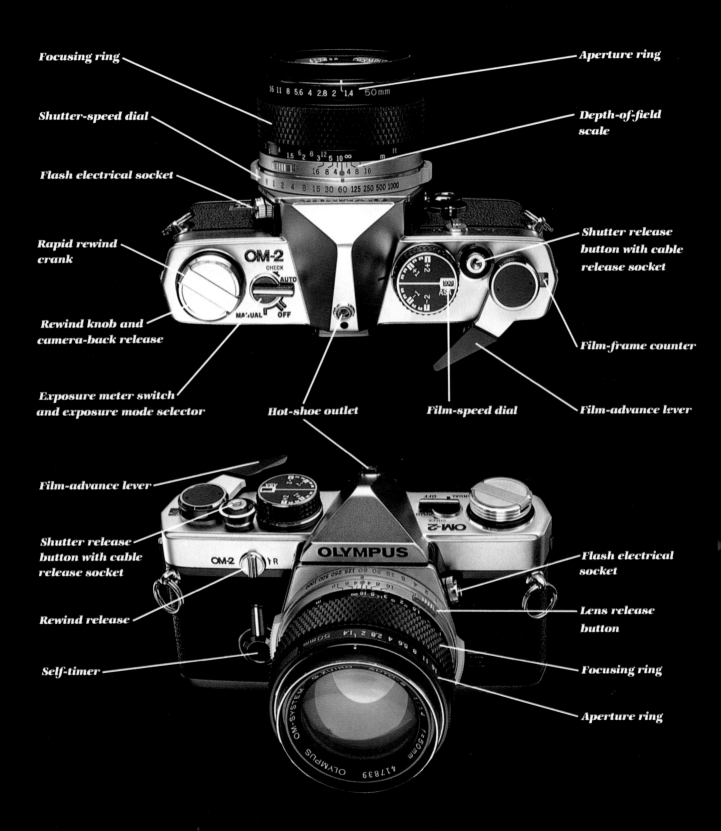

Focusing ring

Aperture ring

Shutter-speed dial

Depth-of-field scale

Flash electrical socket

Shutter release button with cable release socket

Rapid rewind crank

Rewind knob and camera-back release

Film-frame counter

Exposure meter switch and exposure mode selector

Hot-shoe outlet

Film-speed dial

Film-advance lever

Film-advance lever

Shutter release button with cable release socket

Flash electrical socket

Rewind release

Lens release button

Self-timer

Focusing ring

Aperture ring

Exposure Systems

Conventionally correct exposure produces a picture that depicts the subject with a familiar range of tones. All but the lightest and darkest areas retain some detail, and middle tones separate the extremes. But if your aim is interpretation rather than literal recording, a correct exposure renders the subject the way you want it to look.

Photographic exposure is a balancing act in which you use an exposure meter, or light meter, to measure the amount of available light, to relate it to the sensitivity of the film, and to express the relationship as a combination of aperture (in *f*-stops) and shutter speed (in seconds). Your first step in determining exposure is to set the film-speed dial for the ISO/ASA rating of your film, a numerical expression of the film's sensitivity to light. The larger the number, the greater the sensitivity, and the greater the film's sensitivity, the less exposure required.

In relating light to film sensitivity, a camera's light meter may indicate a single combination of shutter speed and lens aperture, or it may present a wide range of equivalent pairs. An exposure of 1/1000 second at *f*/2, for example, can produce an exposure equivalent to 1/15 second at *f*/16. Each time you double the exposure time by dropping to the next slower shutter speed, you can halve the amount of light passing through the lens by closing the aperture one full *f*-stop to maintain the overall balance. Halving the exposure time by selecting a faster shutter speed would require opening the lens aperture one full stop to compensate. Your choice depends on the requirements of your subject and the way you want to portray it. For example, to stop the action of a moving subject, you'll need a fast shutter speed, such as 1/1000 or 1/500 second, and the appropriate aperture. But if good depth of field (see page 38) is your priority, you'll need a small lens aperture, such as *f*/22 or *f*/16, and whatever shutter speed is needed.

Most meters are calibrated to assume that all subjects consist of roughly equal amounts of light and dark tones that average out to medium grey. If you put the average outdoor scene on a sunny day into a huge blender, the resulting mixture would be an 18 percent grey. Because a meter "thinks" all subjects are 18 percent grey, the exposure data it presents are intended to render whatever it reads as 18 percent grey. If your

subject is noticeably lighter or darker than middle grey, you will have to correct the meter's recommendations accordingly. For example, a predominantly light subject, such as a white stucco house on a white sand beach, will require about a stop more exposure than the meter indicates to record as a textured white rather than a grey tone. Conversely, the proverbial black cat in a coal bin would need about a stop less exposure than the meter recommends. Stay alert to subject characteristics so you'll be ready to outthink your meter when necessary.

Another way to solve unusual exposure problems is to make a substitute

A normal prime lens on a 35 mm camera has the exposure controls at the photographer's fingertips. From bottom are the aperture ring, depth-of-field scale, and focusing ring.

Richard Grese

Overexposure

Correct exposure

Underexposure

Dennis Hallinan

When photographing a sunrise or sunset, you might want to deliberately underexpose the scene to produce a rich-colored sky and silhouetted foreground. To determine exposure for such an interpretation when the foreground is fairly large, meter only the brightest part of the sky.

Richard Frear

Sunlight streaking through the latticework wall of an old barn created an unusual pattern of highlights and shadows. Because exposure was based on the darker areas of the interior, some of the highlights are considerably overexposed and, as a result, interestingly flared.

reading by aiming the meter at a similarly illuminated target that has more normal tones than your subject. You can buy an 18 percent grey test card from your photo dealer and carry it in your equipment bag. Or you can make a reading from the palm of your hand, and give one stop more exposure than the meter indicates by opening the lens aperture *or* using a slower shutter speed. On a bright, sunny day, a deep blue, clear sky is a good reference for setting exposure, too. Reading blue sky is approximately equivalent to reading a grey card.

You can deliberately change a theoretically correct exposure for creative results. Setting the camera for less exposure than the meter suggests will darken the picture overall. Giving more than the metered exposure will lighten the finished picture. Underexposing tends to reveal more detail in highlight areas while losing detail in shadowed parts. Overexposing does the opposite. As a starting point for your own creativity, consider that predominantly dark-toned subjects take on a heavy, brooding quality when underexposed, whereas primarily light-toned subjects look delicate and ethereal when moderately overexposed. When you are facing unusual subject characteristics or striving for uncommon exposure effects, bracket your calculated exposure by taking shots a stop or two over and under. With black-and-white film, bracket in full-stop increments. In color, bracket in half-stops.

Occasionally, you may be unable to obtain a useful meter response because the light is too dim or the subject too dark. If so, meter a clean white card or sheet of paper and give about two and one-half stops more exposure than the meter indicates. Or you can try resetting the meter's ISO/ASA speed dial to double or quadruple the actual film speed, and then give one or two stops more exposure, respectively, than the meter indicates. This method is helpful when the meter senses enough light but is incapable of presenting the readout because of design limitations. If you use this method, be sure to reset the film-speed dial to the proper value after you are finished with that exposure situation.

The Automatic Camera

In the past few years, technology has produced newer models of the SLR camera that have sophisticated automatic exposure systems, as well as improved designs for manually operated cameras. These different camera designs offer you different degrees of assistance in setting exposure and different levels of control over your subject. In a manual model, it is up to you to adjust the aperture or shutter speed or both until the meter indicates a "correct" exposure. Manual cameras are slightly slower to operate when you encounter rapidly changing light levels. On the other hand, you are always free to follow or modify their exposure suggestions.

Automatic cameras meter a subject and provide proper exposure as perceived by the meter. Because they respond almost instantly to changes in light level, they are fast to use, and they relieve you of routine exposure-setting chores in most normal situations. You can spend more time concentrating on the subject, less on adjusting the camera. However, when you determine that special exposure techniques are necessary in order to compensate for unusual conditions or to produce special effects, you must disengage the camera's auto-exposure system or trick it into doing what you wish.

The three basic automatic exposure systems are aperture-priority, shutter-priority, and programmed. Aperture-priority systems require you to set the lens aperture while the camera automatically picks a compatible shutter speed, varying it as necessary in response to changing light levels. Shutter-priority systems let you set the shutter speed you desire, while the camera adjusts the lens aperture. In programmed automation, the camera adjusts both shutter speed and lens aperture, sometimes simultaneously, sometimes alternately, depending on the specific design. Many automatic cameras also provide a manual mode in which you have full control over shutter speed and aperture. A few advanced models let you choose one of several automatic modes or manual operation.

Aperture-priority cameras are especially convenient for controlling depth of field, but you must keep an eye on the automatically set shutter speed when photographing action. When you wish to set a specific shutter speed, simply think of the aperture control as a shutter-speed selector: turn it until the camera sets the shutter speed you want. With a shutter-priority automatic camera, you can select whatever shutter speed you need to render motion as you wish, sharp or blurred, and it won't change when the brightness of the scene changes. The lens aperture will change, however, and with it, the depth of field. When you want to set a specific lens aperture for depth-of-field control, use the shutter-speed dial as an aperture selector: simply turn it until the camera sets the lens opening you want.

Cameras using aperture- or shutter-priority systems usually indicate in the viewfinder the shutter speed or f-stop, respectively. Watch these indicators to avoid surprises. If your camera does not indicate the automatically set shutter speed and f-stop, consult the owner's manual to learn what exposure combinations are likely to be set under various shooting conditions with film in the speed range you normally use. If you suspect you will need relatively fast shutter speeds and small apertures, use a high-speed film with an ISO/ASA rating of 400.

The easiest way to make corrected or creative exposures with an automatic camera is to switch it to the manual operating mode, if the design permits. This mode allows you to set any shutter speed/f-stop combination you want. Many automatic SLRs provide an exposure compensation, or override, control that allows you to get up to two stops more or less exposure than the meter recommends. You set the control for the adjustment you want, and the automatic exposure system continues to operate, protecting you from unnoticed changes in light intensity. When you use the override, make a point of resetting it to the normal position as soon as it is no longer needed.

If your automatic camera doesn't have an override or a manual mode, you can make it provide specific degrees of over- or underexposure by tricking the meter. Change the film-speed setting to a higher number to induce underexposure or to a lower number for overexposure. For example, with film rated at ISO/ASA 200, setting the meter at 400 would cause one stop less exposure than normal, and setting it at 100 would result in one stop more exposure than normal. Make sure you reset the film-speed dial at the proper value.

There exists an extensive array of 35 mm cameras to cover nearly any photographic challenge. There are models with both manual and automatic exposure control, through-the-lens and rangefinder focusing or automatic focusing, plus compact designs to fit into your pocket. You can also get cameras with specially designed housings for underwater picture taking.

Depth of Field

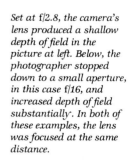
John Phelps

Set at f/2.8, the camera's lens produced a shallow depth of field in the picture at left. Below, the photographer stopped down to a small aperture, in this case f/16, and increased depth of field substantially. In both of these examples, the lens was focused at the same distance.

When you focus a lens to form a sharp image, a zone of sharpness is created that extends in front of and behind the main subject plane. This zone of sharpness is called the depth of field, and the way you use it can drastically alter the content or mood of a photograph. An extremely shallow zone of sharpness lets you soften foreground and background details that might clutter the image. On the other hand, great sharpness in depth lets you pack much information or texture into a single picture.

The basic factors affecting depth of field are lens aperture, focusing distance, and image size on film. If all other factors are constant, depth of field increases as the lens aperture decreases. Large apertures yield shallow depth of field, and smaller apertures extend the sharp zone. If the lens aperture remains constant, depth of field decreases as the focusing distance decreases, and increases as the focusing distance increases. Thus, the closer you are to your subject, the less depth of field you will have at a given f-stop.

If you change the image size on film – by switching from a wide-angle lens, for example, to a telephoto lens – the depth of field also changes. At a given f-stop and focusing distance, depth of field decreases as the image size on film increases. For example, a telephoto lens, which makes a large image on film, will yield less depth of field than a normal or wide-angle lens, which makes a smaller image.

With SLR cameras, you can see the depth of field on the viewing screen much as it will appear on film by using the camera's depth-of-field preview mechanism. Modern SLRs normally present a viewing/focusing image formed at the lens's largest aperture for maximum brightness, and the aperture closes down automatically to the selected setting when you trip the shutter. The preview mechanism lets you close the lens to the set aperture before the exposure so you can judge depth of field on the viewing screen. The image becomes dim when the aperture is reduced, but if you peer into the finder for several seconds, your eye should adapt well enough for you to gain a useful impression of the sharpness in depth.

When the viewing image is too dark to judge satisfactorily, or if you use a camera that doesn't offer SLR viewing and focusing, you can estimate depth of field with the depth-of-field scale that customarily appears on the lens barrel. The scale consists of a central focusing index flanked by distance markers for different lens apertures. After focusing, find the markers on the depth-of-field scale for the f-stop you wish to use. Then read the distances indicated on the distance scale. Those distances are the near and far limits of the zone of acceptable sharpness.

If you like to limit depth of field by using a large aperture, you'll sometimes find yourself unable to use a large enough aperture in bright surroundings. One way to solve that problem is by using neutral density filters (see page 202). Unfortunately, no filter can increase the light flow through the lens when you want all the depth of field you can get. Your only options then are to lengthen shutter speeds or increase the amount of light illuminating the subject. If you know in advance that you will want both fast shutter speeds and great depth of field, use a high-speed film to better your chances.

Ernst Haas

Ernst Haas used a large
lens aperture on a
telephoto lens to produce
a shallow depth of field so
only the boy would be in
sharp focus.

Keith Boas

To record both the
foreground and
background of this
Arizona view in sharp
focus, a small aperture of
f/16 was used.

Motion

An important creative element in photography is the depiction of motion. Although the term *still photography* implies the absence of movement, most subjects do move to some extent. And you can record this motion as you wish, depending on the shutter speed you select or induce an automatic camera to set. A high shutter speed such as 1/1000 second allows you to capture most moving subjects on film so sharply that they appear frozen in space. Slower shutter speeds allow motion to blur on film, softening detail but often enhancing the impression of speed.

One form of motion blur generally to avoid is caused by camera movement. You'll win half the battle by applying gentle pressure to the shutter release rather than jabbing it. Another important safeguard is to use a shutter speed fast enough to negate the effects of unavoidable body movement. Here's a handy formula for determining the slowest shutter speed it's safe to use: place the number 1 over the focal length of the lens, expressed in millimetres, and consider the fraction as a shutter speed. The focal length (see page 42) is usually engraved on the retaining ring encircling the front element or elsewhere on the lens barrel. With a 50 mm lens, 1/50 second would be the slowest shutter speed at which you could reasonably expect to avoid image degradation from camera movement. Since 1/60 second is the nearest marked speed on most cameras, that would be the slowest safe speed to set.

To freeze a moving subject, select the fastest shutter speed that will still permit proper exposure. With an aperture-priority automatic camera, open the lens aperture until the shutter speed reaches the desired setting. If you know in advance that you will be photographing fast-moving subjects, load your camera with a high-speed film. That way you'll be able to use fast shutter speeds without having to open the lens aperture so much that you're hampered by insufficient depth of field. If there isn't enough light to use fast shutter speeds, you can use an electronic flash to record moving subjects sharply as long as they are within effective range of the flash (see page 164). Don't use flash, however, if it might distract athletes, performers, or other spectators.

Sometimes you will want to make a more expressive picture by letting a moving

Neil Montanus

A hand-held camera was panned with this woman as she walked along a Brazilian street. A slow shutter speed of 1/15 second combined with the camera movement to produce the blurred background.

subject record as a blur or streak. This approach can be especially effective in color. With a hand-held camera, set a shutter speed fast enough to negate camera movement but slow enough to let the moving subject blur. Frame the area where the action is occurring and hold the camera steady during the exposure. Stationary elements in the scene will record sharply while the moving subject blurs. If you mount the camera on a tripod, you can use exposures as long as you wish to achieve the desired degree of motion blur. If you have an aperture-priority camera, selecting small f-stops such as $f/16$ and $f/22$ will elicit relatively slow shutter speeds. To obtain extreme blur effects with long time exposures, switch the camera to manual mode and set the shutter on B. Choose a

Joseph R. May

In Tampa, Florida, the old Bayview Hotel is "frozen" in its dying seconds with a shutter speed of 1/1000 second and a 200 mm telephoto lens.

Using a camera on a tripod and a slow (1/15 second or slower) shutter speed, you can make rushing water, such as this waterfall in Three Sisters Wilderness Area, Oregon, take on a delicate, smoky appearance.

Ed Cooper

slow-speed film to make unusually long exposures. In bright conditions, a neutral density filter helps reduce further the light entering the camera (see page 202).

A valuable technique for conveying a strong impression of speed is panning, in which you track the moving subject through the viewfinder during the exposure (see page 158). When done well, panning results in a picture in which the moving subject is rendered fairly sharply, but the foreground and background are streaked. Panning works best with subjects moving directly across your field of view. Shutter speeds from about 1/60 to 1/8 second or so generally produce interesting effects. However, you'll have to experiment to determine the shutter speeds that produce effects you like with your chosen subjects and circumstances. Medium- and slow-speed films facilitate working in a slow shutter-speed range; and, again, neutral density filters can help if the light is exceptionally bright.

Until you've developed a sense of which shutter speeds render motion to your taste, photograph each situation several times at different settings and record the data for later reference. With a manual camera, remember to reset the lens aperture accordingly when you change shutter speed.

Perspective

The position from which you photograph a subject has an important effect on the resulting image. Close up or far away, looking up, down, or sideways, you can alter the impact and mood of your subject. The two principal means of making these creative changes are your lens and your angle of view.

A lens is measured in focal length, which is the effective distance, usually expressed in millimetres, between it and the film when the lens is focused at infinity. Normal lenses for 35 mm cameras have focal lengths ranging from 45 mm to 55 mm. The normal lens approximates the angle of view of normal human vision, producing pictures that include about as much of a scene as you see at any given moment. Spatial relationships between objects within the field generally look familiar, too.

Lenses of focal lengths up to 45 mm are called wide-angle lenses, and they record more of a scene at any given distance than normal lenses. Because a wide-angle lens squeezes more of a scene onto a fixed film area, individual elements are recorded smaller than when photographed at the same distance with a normal lens. Distance and size relationships of picture elements often appear unnatural at close shooting distances, with the nearest objects looking abnormally large, and slightly more distant ones looking disproportionately small and far.

Lenses of focal lengths longer than 55 mm are telephoto lenses. The opposite of wide-angle lenses, telephoto lenses include less subject area than a normal lens, but each detail within the lens field is enlarged on film. Distances between objects in the scene often appear compressed, and size relationships may be distorted. In extreme cases, objects of quite different sizes may look nearly the same size on film.

Ultra-wide-angle and very long telephoto lenses are available. Fisheye lenses are 6 to 17 mm in focal length and are designed for radical wide-field coverage. As a consequence, they produce curved representations of straight lines in the image. At the other end of the focal-length range are mirror, or catadioptric, lenses in which high-precision mirrors fold the internal light path so that the image magnification is obtained with a lens that is much shorter and more compact than its focal length would indicate.

You can use interchangeable lenses

Lens manufacturers offer hundreds of accessory lenses for 35 mm single-lens reflex cameras.

Pictured here are focal lengths ranging from an ultra-wide-angle to a mirror telephoto lens.

two distinct ways to influence the appearance of your pictures. One way is to adjust your image size by changing focal length instead of changing camera-to-subject distance. A more imaginative use, though, is to change focal length to maintain a desired image size on film when you are changing distance or vantage point in order to alter perspective.

In photography, perspective refers to the appearance of three-dimensional subjects as rendered on a two-dimensional piece of film. It is a function of camera-to-subject distance and camera viewpoint, not lens focal length. If you take a series of pictures of the same scene from the same distance with lenses ranging from wide-angle to telephoto, the image size on film will increase with each jump in focal length, but the perspective will remain the same. The relative sizes of objects within the scene will be constant.

If you were to take a series of pictures of the same subject from different distances, size relationships and apparent distances between various objects within the scene would change from one picture to another – whether you used only one lens for

200 mm telephoto lens

105 mm telephoto lens

28 mm wide-angle lens

17 mm full-frame fisheye lens

8 mm, 180-degree fisheye lens

Robert Phillips

For exaggerated keystoning in this Las Vegas street scene, the photographer used a wide-angle lens and a low viewing angle –tilting his camera upward, away from vertical lines in the scene.

the series or changed lenses with each distance change to maintain the same image size of the principal subject. In the latter case, the principal subject would be the same size in each frame of film, but details at nearer and farther distances would not be matched in size from frame to frame because of changing perspective. Wide-angle lenses let you change perspective by exaggerating the size of foreground objects relative to farther elements because they permit picture taking from closer than normal distances. Long telephoto lenses tend to reduce apparent size differences and distances of various objects within the field by compelling you to photograph at greater camera-to-subject distances.

Another determinant of perspective is camera placement relative to the subject. Photographing from a low angle or a high one can cause distortion in your subject (see pages 82 and 84). This phenomenon occurs when the film in the camera isn't parallel to the surface of your subject. It is more noticeable in pictures made with short focal lengths at close distances than in telephoto shots made at greater distances. And it is most apparent as a convergence, called keystoning, in which straight parallel lines appear to converge in the photograph.

A telephoto lens compressed the distance in this scene of a Scouting jamboree to accent the similarity of shapes between the images of sails and tents.

Cary Wolinsky

Natural Light

Natural light is such a customary part of our lives that the human eye functions well in midday sun, deep shade, heavy overcast, and even moonlight. We accept changes in the quality of natural light without a second thought. But successful photography demands that we pay closer attention because, after the subject, light is the most important component of a photograph. It determines how the subject will look in terms of contour, form, texture, tone, and color.

Hardness and softness are qualities of light that depend both on general weather conditions and on specific subject location relative to the sun or other light sources. Hard light is brilliant direct illumination produced by the sun on a clear day, and it creates bright highlights and intense, clearly defined shadows. Soft or diffused light is typified by the enveloping illumination of an overcast day or a large area of shade. Highlights may differ little from middle tones, and shadows are soft-edged or nonexistent. Soft lighting is excellent for photographing people because it doesn't exaggerate complexion flaws.

The direction from which light falls on the subject is also important. Although you cannot move the sun, you can move your subject or your camera to produce a better effect. And you can choose times of day when the sun illuminates your subject as you wish.

Frontlighting, in which the sun is behind the camera and floods the scene evenly with light, is easy to work with. Shadows are minimal, and subjects can move about freely. The trade-off is that frontlighting tends to look flat, robbing pictures of the illusion of depth and washing out delicate textures.

Sidelighting, in which the sun skims across the surface of the subject facing the lens, emphasizes texture and form. Numerous shadows are evident and may themselves be prominent design elements. If there is a great difference in brightness between highlight and shadow areas, you may wish to adjust exposure to emphasize detail in either darker or lighter portions of the scene. One stop more exposure than your meter indicates will preserve shadow detail, although possibly at the expense of overexposing highlight areas. One stop less exposure than the meter indicates will reduce the risk of burning out highlight detail but

Manlin Maureen Chee Forgay

Soft diffused light from an open window or door provides flattering illumination for portraits.

may sacrifice some detail in shadows.

Backlighting is dramatic, with the sun behind the subject, creating a halo-like rim of light and casting pronounced shadows. Backlighting augments the illusion of depth in landscapes because the shadows separate planes effectively. It can also evoke a dreamy, romantic mood in portraits. Exposure effects in backlighting can range from a full silhouette of the subject that shows detail only in the highlights to a rendition revealing full detail in the shadowed areas with glaring, burned-out highlights. If you want detail in the shadows, read exposure from a significant shadow area while shielding the meter from direct rays of the sun.

Kelvin units are the measurement for describing the color of light: the lower the

Candace Cochrane

The striking backdrop of an exiting storm, complete with a faint rainbow, gave impact to this photograph in Newfoundland. Direct sunlight, breaking through the cloud cover, provided dramatic contrast between the pastoral foreground and the sinister sky.

George Elich

An overcast day produces soft, nearly shadowless illumination, presenting an ideal condition for photographing appealing tonal gradations.

color temperature, the redder the light; and the higher the color temperature, the bluer the light. The "white" light of standard daylight has a color temperature of 5500 K and is actually quite blue. A warmly tinted sunrise or sunset might have a color temperature of about 3100 K or lower. Daylight two hours past sunrise or two hours before sunset is approximately 4000 K. An overcast sky produces cool-toned light from 6500 to 9000 K, and open shade may be bathed in distinctly bluish light with a color temperature well above 12,000 K. Take advantage of natural variations in daylight to influence color rendition in your pictures.

Choosing a film for daylight photography is a matter of both technical requirements and aesthetic preference. One clear-cut choice concerns color temperatures and the color transparency, or slide, films that are manufactured with reduced sensitivity to blue to compensate for the high color temperatures of normal daylight. If you expose an indoor, or tungsten, color slide film in daylight, the result will be excessive blueness. General-purpose color negative films are compatible with daylight, as are black-and-white films.

An important consideration in picking any film is its sensitivity to light, which bears directly on your ability to stop action and to obtain depth of field. On a bright, sunny day, high-speed films rated at ISO/ASA 400 let you shoot at 1/500 second at f/16 in bright areas and 1/250 second at f/4 in the shade. A medium-speed film at ISO/ASA 125 allows you to use settings of 1/125 second at f/16 in bright areas and 1/60 at f/4 in the shade. Slow-speed films at ISO/ASA 25 let you shoot at 1/30 at f/16 and 1/30 at f/2.8 under the same respective conditions.

45

Artificial Light

Photography by artificial light differs in several important respects from photographing in daylight. Usually the light level is much lower, often there are multiple light sources, and, if you're taking color pictures, you have to match the film to the light source or use a filter to obtain realistic color rendition.

Because most artificial illumination is comparatively dim, you should use fast films with ISO/ASA ratings of 160 or higher for hand-held picture taking and to stop action. When relatively long exposure times are feasible, you can use a tripod and slower films. When there are several light sources in the scene, appraise the lighting effect carefully. If each object casts a confusing tangle of shadows, either change your camera position or framing to exclude them, or turn off enough lights to simplify the lighting. Try to avoid including light sources in the scene if they are likely to create distracting "hot spots" or flare.

Many artificial light sources have color temperatures much lower than that of standard daylight. They produce light that contains more red and less blue. Typical examples are tungsten-filament household lamps, which usually range from about 2800 K to 3000 K; 3200 K professional studio lamps; and 3400 K photolamps. If you expose daylight color slide films under such illumination, the results will have an orange tint. Although you could use a light-balancing or conversion filter to alter the color of the light entering the camera, the resulting loss in effective film speed would be undesirable. Instead, select a film balanced to produce plausible color with the dominant light source. Kodak tungsten-balanced (type B) slide films such as Ektachrome 160 film (tungsten) produce excellent color quality with 3200 K and similar light sources. Kodachrome 40 film, 5070 (type A), is balanced for use with 3400 K photolamps. Both type A and type B films work satisfactorily with ordinary household lamps, producing slightly warm but attractive color rendition. Color negative materials such as Kodacolor 400 and Kodacolor II film, although daylight-balanced, may be used with tungsten lighting because corrective filtration can be introduced in printing. For more accurate rendition, however, use a No. 80A filter over the lens with 3200 K lamps or

John Olson

a No. 80B with 3400 K photolamps.

Fluorescent tubes commonly used in home, industrial, and commercial lighting are not directly compatible with any specific type of color film. Daylight slide films are generally preferable to tungsten-balanced films under fluorescent lights, but they tend to produce yellow-green results. More neutral rendition may be obtained by using an FLD filter over the lens. When photographing by fluorescent illumination, use shutter speeds slower than 1/60 second to avoid unexpected color casts and underexposure.

Carbon-arc lighting, which is often encountered at sporting events and entertainment spectaculars, is easy to handle photographically. It has a color temperature in the range of 5000 K to 5500 K and yields good color with daylight color films.

High-intensity discharge lamps, such as the mercury-vapor type used to light many streets and parking lots at night, yield extremely off-color results with color slide films unless you use a filter. Or you can use a color negative film such as Kodacolor 400 or Kodacolor II film and apply filters during printing to correct the color.

When the ambient light is photographically unacceptable or inconvenient to correct, electronic flash provides a practical alternative. Its brief duration, usually 1/1000 second or shorter, and color temperature in the area of 5500 K allow you to stop even rapid action effectively and produce good color quality with

Warm-colored footlights add to the holiday atmosphere in this picture photographed by existing light. For dimly lighted interiors, such as stage shows, where flash might not carry far enough to light your subject adequately, use a camera with an f/2.8 or faster lens and a high-speed, tungsten-balanced color film.

Frank Siteman

For a natural quality in photographs, take pictures by existing light. Here candles provided the only illumination, and daylight-balanced film added a further note of warm tone.

daylight-balanced film. At reasonably close flash-to-subject distances, even small units generate enough light to overpower and negate the effects of ambient illumination. In exchange for these advantages, though, you do lose the mood evoked by the existing light.

As a rule, mixing light sources of grossly different color temperatures creates an insoluble problem in terms of achieving plausible color rendition. If you select a film or filter to match the color quality of one light source, only the portion of the scene lighted by that source will display proper color balance. Areas lighted by other sources will show color casts. If you must photograph in color under mixed lighting, either overpower the area lighting with flash to achieve uniform color quality or try to turn off all but the most desirable lights. For example, in a room flooded by natural light coming through windows and by strong tungsten lighting, you have two obvious possibilities. Turn off the room lights and take the pictures on daylight film, or draw the blinds and use a tungsten-balanced film. In any case, though, don't overlook the possibility of using mixed lighting intentionally to achieve unusual but attractive color effects.

Ellis Herwig

Photographing under fluorescent illumination on daylight-balanced film without a filter lends an appropriate yellow-green cast to this scene.

Color

Patty Van Dolson

We tend to attribute the colors we see to the objects we're viewing. In fact, colors originate with the light illuminating the objects. For example, daylight is a blend of all the visible wavelengths of the spectrum. When daylight illuminates something in our field of view, our eyes detect the light the object reflects. If the object reflects all or nearly all the light, we perceive it as white. If it reflects little or none of the light, we perceive it as black. And if it absorbs some wavelengths of light and reflects others, we see it as whatever color or combination of colors it reflects. An apple looks red because it reflects red wavelengths.

Color is important in the photographs we make. A boldly colored subject against a neutral or subdued background becomes dramatically prominent. Red, orange, and yellow are associated with warmth and appear to advance toward the viewer. Blues and greens signal coolness and seem to recede. You can strongly influence the way viewers respond to a picture by choosing carefully the colors that predominate and controlling the relationships among the various colors in the scene.

Photographs in which colors are rendered realistically are frequently accepted as literal representations of the subject, even when minor color discrepancies exist. This acceptance occurs because the human eye is not very good at remembering exact colors, even though it is a sensitive instrument for comparing colors viewed side by side. In direct color comparisons, the eye detects subtle differences with ease. If you wish to produce color abstractions, you can leave realism behind by making pictures with strong overall color casts or in which specific objects of known color are shown in unexpected hues. You can alter color balance by deliberately mismatching film and light source or by placing a filter of the desired color over the lens. Showing part of a scene realistically and other parts imaginatively can be done with lighting if you illuminate the part of the scene you want to show literally with light matched to the film, and illuminate other areas with light of incompatible balance.

If you make long exposures with general-purpose color films, as in still-life or night photography, you are likely to encounter a phenomenon known as failure of the law of reciprocity, or the reciprocity effect. It can also occasionally occur at extremely short exposure times. The law of reciprocity states that a given level of exposure may be achieved with equal success by exposing the film to bright light for a short time or to dim light for a long time. Unfortunately, the theory does not apply when very short or very long exposures are involved.

The reciprocity effect manifests itself with color film as underexposure, usually accompanied by a color shift. The degree of underexposure and color shift usually increases as exposure time increases. When you anticipate the need for long exposures, consult the film instruction sheet to determine the filtration and additional exposure required for the exposure time you are using. Usually, it is better to increase the exposure by opening the lens aperture rather than by further lengthening the exposure time, which can worsen the problem.

The variety of films available for 35 mm cameras can be divided into three basic types: those yielding black-and-white negatives, those yielding color negatives, and those yielding color slides. Information on a box of film indicates the type and color balance, film speed, number of exposures, and date by which you should have it processed.

Dante Russo

Here a split-field filter (see page 200) provided extra color in the land area while a CCO5M gelatin filter added a slight magenta tint overall.

This eerie photograph was made by exposing Kodak Ektachrome infrared film through a No. 12 filter and deliberately underexposing to achieve the silhouette.

Frank Siteman

In some cases, you may be able to sidestep the reciprocity effect by switching to a more sensitive film that allows shorter exposure times. Another possibility is to use flash rather than relatively weak continuous light. Still another option is "pushing" the speed of the film.

Pushing, or push-processing, consists of exposing a roll of film as though it were more sensitive than it is and then extending development time to compensate for the resulting underexposure. For example, Ektachrome 400 film can be exposed as though its speed rating were 800 instead of 400 and then be push-processed instead of developed normally. All 135-size and roll Ektachrome films can be pushed successfully by one full stop. That is, you may expose them at double the published ISO/ASA rating. You must expose the entire roll at the same film speed and tell the processing laboratory that the film requires special development to compensate for the one-stop push.

The colors you photograph, whether they are soft pastels or bright, saturated hues, have the power to inspire subtle reactions. Choose your colors carefully to establish or reinforce the mood. In this example, the prominent display of red and yellow suggests a cheerful, festive atmosphere.

Black and White

In contrast to the familiar look of a conventional color photograph, a black-and-white picture carries the viewer immediately into the realm of abstraction. Because it renders colors as light or dark shades of grey, giving its subjects new visual identities, black-and-white film is at its best when used to interpret rather than merely record. It is superb at capturing patterns and contrasts, textures and forms, and all manner of tonal relationships, from the most powerful to the most subtle.

Film characteristics to consider are sharpness, graininess, and contrast. Sharpness is a film's ability to render detail crisply. As a rule, slower films are slightly sharper than high-speed films. Graininess is the granular texture of the enlarged image, and it is generally less apparent with slow-speed films. Contrast refers to the way a film records subject tones, with contrasty materials exaggerating differences between light and dark areas. All of these qualities influence the way the final image will look.

Kodak general-purpose black-and-white films are available in a wide range of sensitivities, from Panatomic-X film at ISO/ASA 32 to Kodak recording film 2475, with speed ratings from 1000 to 3200, depending on exposure and processing. All may be used in daylight or artificial light without adjustment. Recording film 2475 is noticeably coarser-grained than less sensitive films, but it permits successful hand-held photography without flash in extremely dim existing-light conditions. Its obvious graininess can be an attribute when you want to create a textured effect for aesthetic reasons.

Panatomic-X film is a logical choice when you have ample light or can use a tripod and wish to produce extremely sharp, fine-grain images. Plus-X pan film, ISO/ASA 125, is fast enough for all-around outdoor photography with a hand-held camera and is close enough to Panatomic-X in sharpness and freedom from graininess to use for still lifes or other picture-taking situations when greater depth of field or shorter shutter speeds are desired. Tri-X pan film, ISO/ASA 400, has earned a secure place in the cameras of professional photographers and photohobbyists for combining convenient high speed with sharpness. And it effectively withstands pushing to speeds of 800 to 1200

M. Keith Macdonald

All of the elements within this scene were reduced to varying tones of grey through the application of black-and-white photography. Yet the absence of color has not injured the visual effect.

when you need more film speed than 400 but don't feel compelled to invoke the extreme sensitivity of 2475 recording film.

For the ultimate in abstraction in black and white, Kodak high-speed infrared film can produce eerie landscapes in which deciduous foliage is rendered silvery white and blue skies become almost black. Although intended primarily for scientific and industrial use, this unusual film lends itself to creative applications as diverse as the photographers who conceive them. For more information about this film, see page 220.

Although black-and-white films transmute a world of color into shades of grey, they are sensitive to colors. This sensitivity lets you alter the way the films render colors by mounting colored filters in front of the lens. You can make a color record as a lighter grey by using a filter of similar color, and you can darken the rendition by using a filter of complementary color. For example, a red filter would make a red rose record very light and the green leaves surrounding it very dark.

Stanley Klimek

Kurt Gerber

This double portrait, made on high-speed infrared film, illustrates the film's ability to yield images having a compelling, unearthly quality.

Graininess is a common characteristic of high-speed black-and-white film. Using soft window light for illumination, the photographer made an exposure of 1/60 second at f/5.6.

Karen King

In overcast lighting conditions, fast shutter speeds are required to stop action, so a fast-speed black-and-white film is helpful.

51

Part III

100 Techniques for More Creative Photographs

Shapes

An almost foolproof formula for creating a photograph that immediately catches a viewer's eye is to give priority to a single visual element. Shapes, especially, can be striking. We generally think of shape as the outline created by an object, whether it be the smooth, spherical shape offered by a porcelain doorknob or the detailed shape of a human profile. When shapes become, in essence, the subject of a photograph, the picture assumes both a visual power and an abstract quality. Strong geometrical shapes, such as the ones highlighted in the pictures here, are often the most arresting. The circles and triangles provide a dramatic contrast to the rectangular frame of the photograph.

To make shapes prominent, you must zero in on them with your camera, eliminating busy and distracting background details. And for maximum impact, it is vital that there be a strong contrast between the shapes and the surroundings that define them. This contrast can be between lightness and darkness, as in the photograph of tents at right, or it can come from a difference in color, as in the picture of the white doorknob on a red door. In emphasizing shape, your camera angle is also crucial. In general, a frontal, straight-on angle that minimizes the three-dimensionality of the subject is the one that will produce a flat, distinctive shape on film.

A shape, of course, need not stand in singular splendor. But when encountering a scene that contains two or more similar shapes, it is usually a good idea to crop one of the shapes into a reinforcing echo, as the photographers have done in the shots of tents and ship funnels.

Strong sidelighting from a late afternoon sun turns an encampment of tents into an intriguing patchwork of contrasting dark and pastel triangles.

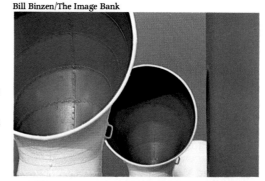

With their dark green interiors crisply outlined by white rims, ventilation funnels on a ship deck become a study of overlapping circles. By showing part rather than all of the foreground funnel, the photographer obtained a much tighter composition.

Light from one side reveals the natural, curving shape of a leaf's tip against a dark background. The waterdrops accentuate its texture and form.

▶
Many common objects become powerful, even puzzling, shapes when photographed from a straight-on angle that flattens their three-dimensional appearance. Here, only the keyhole tells us that the circular shape above it is a doorknob.

Peter A. Torrente

Lines

Good photographers often use lines in their pictures to direct the viewer's attention to the main subject. They also recognize that lines can create a sense of depth or show movement in a picture. The innovative photographer will find that when lines themselves become the subject, the effect can be stunning. It doesn't matter whether the lines are straight or curved, or whether they draw the eye into the image or lead it away. What is important is that the lines be dynamic.

To arouse the viewer's interest, lines must convey a sense of motion, as do the red diagonals in the shot of a hotel lobby and the dramatically undulating curve in the picture of a dune. By contrast, horizontal and vertical lines that run parallel to the edges of the picture are static and, as a result, are the least capable of standing alone. They can, however, be used sparingly to counterpoint more dynamic lines, as the elevator lights do in Peter Turner's picture of the ultra-modern hotel lobby.

In looking for lines to photograph, it is sometimes best to watch how they work with each other, since this interaction can add to the tension the photo captures. At other times it is best to isolate a line or even a portion of a line to increase this tension. Also look for lines at various times of the day; some lines, such as the soft curve of the sand dune, are only dramatically defined when sunlight hits from a low angle, late in the afternoon or early in the morning.

What subject could be more commonplace than the dividing lines in a roadway? Yet by choosing an unusual camera angle, the photographer turns them into bold diagonals cutting across the corner of an almost abstract composition.

The zigzagging lines of this structure would have been too stark to be of interest by themselves. The presence of two figures, however, interrupts the visual monotony and gives us an idea of the stairway's size.

In this photograph of exposed hotel corridors and lighted elevators, photographer Pete Turner achieves a dramatic effect by contrasting converging lines with delicate, light-inscribed verticals.

Patty Van Dolson

The sinuous line of a sand dune conveys a feeling of desert calm while creating dynamic visual interest at the same time.

Patterns

Pattern – the repetition of shapes, lines, or colors – is another visual element that can star as the subject of an eye-catching photograph. As the pictures here demonstrate, we are surrounded by an almost infinite variety of patterns, some the handiwork of nature, others of our own creation. Their regularity instills a pleasing sense of rhythm and harmony in a picture. But too much uniformity can make a photograph visually boring, and the secret to using patterns creatively is to find ones with variations that catch the eye of the viewer. In the picture of Indians, for example, the variety in the colors of the turbans is the factor that makes it interesting.

Generally, pattern photographs are most successful not only when the pattern fills the entire picture, but when the image is also so tightly framed that the pattern seems to extend endlessly beyond the edges of the picture, as the sea of luggage does.

Patterns are usually best revealed by flat, even lighting and a straight-on camera angle, since both tend to make an object appear to have less depth, allowing repeated flat planes to predominate. But this is far from being a hard-and-fast rule, as the picture of the yarn demonstrates.

Tom Carroll/ALPHA

Michael Newler

In a notable exception to the rule that flat, frontal lighting best reveals patterns, the repeated lines of pieces of yarn are shown to advantage by strongly directional sidelighting.

3

The most intriguing patterns are often ones that reveal the diversity of basically similar objects, such as these rows of suitcases in an airport baggage area.

Deanie W. Galloway

Lily pads are a good example of the subtle variations in shape and color that can make natural patterns appealing.

Ric Ergenbright

Crowds of people often provide the most appealing patterns, since there is the added bonus of human interest. The real bonus in this picture taken in India, however, is provided by the brightly colored turbans distributed in an attractive, irregular pattern throughout the group.

Textures

A photograph in which texture predominates can be just as creatively rewarding as one featuring shape or pattern. When emphasized, texture adds realism to a photograph, lending depth and a sense of three-dimensionality to your subjects.

Textures usually become apparent in two very different situations. Some textures are revealed when the photographer moves in close to a subject to magnify its surface irregularities, as in the case of the pictures of the leaf and of the faces here. At the other extreme, textures appear when the photographer backs far away from a large subject and its repetitive surface qualities are revealed, as shown in the photograph of the sun-baked lake bed.

Textures also come alive when light hits a surface at a sharp angle, creating a multiplicity of shadows in the surface's recesses that emphasizes its unevenness. Look at surfaces at different times of day. Horizontal surfaces show their texture best in early morning or late afternoon, when sunlight rakes obliquely across them. Vertical surfaces, on the other hand, are more likely to reveal their textures when the sun is directly overhead.

A successful texture picture should convey to the viewer an impression of how the surface would feel if touched. And as with patterns, the textures that work best offer some visual variety and seem to extend beyond the frame of the picture.

In an extreme close-up, the intricate network of veins and capillaries on the underside of a leaf reveals its delicate texture and subtly contrasting colors.

Rev. E. A. Reuscher

Ken Biggs

The smooth skin of a young child pressed against the face of an elderly woman is a beautiful study in textures as well as a telling image of the passage of time.

Warm light from a setting sun glances across a dried-out lake bottom, emphasizing its cobblestonelike texture. A wide-angle lens increased the picture's sweeping scope.

Composition: Following the Rules

Any mention today of formal rules of composition tends to evoke images of dusty nineteenth-century art academies. And certainly slavish adherence to rigid formulas more often results in pictures that are merely pretty rather than truly original. Yet there is much to be learned from principles that have guided generations of artists, and sometimes a photograph with formal composition can convey its own unique message.

Composition is simply the way that all the elements in a picture are arranged. These elements include lines, shapes, colors, and lightness and darkness. The way you arrange them in your viewfinder will be interpreted later on, so you should organize the ingredients of a scene to achieve your purpose, whether it is to convey a relatively static, quiet mood, as the pictures on these two pages do, or to offer a jarring, eccentric interpretation of a scene or event, as the pictures on pages 64 and 65 do. In a classic composition, there is usually one strong point of interest, or main subject, which first attracts the eye. It can attract us for several reasons: because of its position, because of the subordination of other elements, because it contrasts in color or intensity with its surroundings, or because other elements have been arranged so that they form a frame or path that directs the eye to the subject. After taking in the main subject, the eye may be guided by more subtle indicators to explore subordinate elements.

Overall, a good classic composition has pleasing proportions. There is a balance between light and dark, between massive forms and open space, or between bright and muted colors. Occasionally, if the subject requires it, you may want your composition to be completely symmetrical. But often your pictures will be more dynamic and visually interesting when you place your subject off center. Similarly, a horizon running through the middle of a landscape cuts the picture in two horizontally, creating halves that compete for the viewer's attention. Normally, you should avoid such a dividing line, even if it is vertical. Yet, as the picture of the man and the dog illustrates, when combined with the right balance of colors and camera angle, a strong center line can serve to point up the starkness of a scene.

Despite a strong vertical line separating the man and his dog, they are united by the man's extended arm. The direction of his gaze guides the viewer's eye to the dog.

Angelo Cusati

The problem of having more than one subject of equal importance was cleverly solved in this photo by having two subjects on one side and only one on the other to give the composition a dynamic balance.

▶
Although they are small and take up only a portion of the picture, the child's eyes and hand immediately grab the viewer's attention, boldly interrupting the regular pattern of white Venetian blinds.

Janet Edwards

Composition: Breaking the Rules

Ultimately the most important aspect of a composition is its visual impact—its ability to convey the feeling you want to express in your photograph. Sometimes dramatic impact can be achieved by deliberately ignoring traditional compositional rules or even turning them on end.

A photograph that breaks rules has a certain tension about it. We may see two figures at opposite ends of a beach and wonder what their relationship is, or view a subject that blends into its background because their colors are almost perfectly matched. This tension results when the relationships of elements in a scene are exaggerated—in size, in color, or in the space between them. You can exaggerate by enlarging distances or creating great differences, as in the beach scene below, or you can exaggerate by reducing distances and minimizing differences, as in the two pictures on page 65.

You can also increase tension in a photograph by selectively cropping your subject. Photograph an enigmatic portion of a familiar subject, or capture a moving subject at the edge of the frame, as though it were ready to race off the picture. Properly done, such images can be much more original and creative than ones made by the rules. They can be playful or provocative, startling or seductive. In the end, you have to learn to trust your eyes.

Greg Slater

For visual impact, consider featuring parts of the body as primary photographic subjects. Here a pair of hands becomes part of a striking poolside still life.

Brooke Hummer

Two centers of interest at opposite sides of a picture are usually distracting. But here placement of the subjects so close to the edges in an otherwise deserted setting emphasizes their anonymity and the separateness of their very different activities.

Dr. Edward Leone

A chopped-off subject that fades into its background goes against the conventional rules of composition. Yet by letting the blue of the jeep and the water merge, the photographer has turned this image into an abstract composition of color.

A simple, uncluttered scene and a subject that contrasts with its setting are the usual keys to good picture taking. In this picture, however, the complex pattern of bars and shadows in a zoo cage creates a junglelike atmosphere that echoes the tiger's natural striped camouflage.

Still Lifes: Candid

Photographing still lifes is one of the easiest ways to sharpen your compositional skills while creating original pictures. Still lifes are simply arrangements of inanimate objects. They can be arrangements that the photographer happens upon, like the ones shown here, or they can be groupings carefully set up by the photographer, like the ones shown on pages 68 and 69. The variety of subject matter is limited only by your imagination. Look for still lifes everywhere you go, from your own attic or barn to city streets and secluded beaches.

    The great advantage of still lifes is that they allow you to work at a leisurely pace, giving extra attention to how all the elements work together in the final image. In searching for scenes to photograph, look for combinations that are visually distinctive. The scene can tell a story, as in the picture here of a farmer's hat and jacket. It can display sharply contrasting colors, as in the picture of a basket of apples. Or it can have a subtle interplay of shapes, like the photograph of a broom. Experiment with your camera angle until your scene shows the elements in the most pleasing balance. And don't be afraid to improve upon a scene. Feel free to shift the position of the elements or to eliminate distracting ones. If natural

A scythe forms a frame for a farmer's hat and jacket in this barn still life that is tied together not only by its common rustic theme, but also by the dominance of subtle natural colors.

▶

An unexpected interplay of repeating shapes and colors gives unity to this still life. The shape of the broom is echoed by the yellow cutout on the floor, and that shape, in turn, is echoed by the paint tracings on the wall. At the same time, there is a balance between the predominant yellow and red hues.

lighting is too harsh, as it often is, consider using a reflector or electronic flash to provide supplementary fill-in lighting in shadowy areas.

Baskets reproduced in a uniform shade of blue that makes them look almost artificial provide an effective setting for the natural red and golden hues of apples.

7

Still Lifes: Studio

Photographing a still life in a studio or another controlled setting, rather than photographing an arrangement you happen upon, greatly increases your control over how the final image will look. You take charge not only of selecting and arranging the subject matter, but also of choosing the background, camera angle, and lighting. Professionals often resort to elaborate set-ups – lights, reflectors, diffusers, and special backdrops – for their studio still lifes, which can be seen in magazine ads. But it is best to start simply. A single subject lighted by a single light source against a plain background allows you to experiment greatly with the effects of changing camera and lighting angles.

When you move on to more complex still lifes, simplicity remains the best rule. A yard or two of cloth or of the special background paper known as "no-seam" or "seamless" (available in many art and photo-supply stores) can provide an uncluttered background. A sheet of white cardboard can serve as a reflector to supply soft fill-in light in shadowy areas. A couple of lightweight folding stands for the light and the reflector, along with a tripod for the camera, are all the other equipment you need.

For still-life subjects, simplicity is again important. As the photo of hangers here attests, you don't need to collect a wide range of elaborate objects to create an interesting, handsome picture. When you do want to create a scene, choose objects that have some common thread. As the other pictures here show, food is an easy beginning subject with a common theme. But the subject could just as well be sporting equipment, an artist's materials, or a collection of memorabilia. Think about what interests you and use that as a theme. If your hobby is gardening, you might photograph flowers with some of your gardening tools as props.

The arrangement of a still life should start with the positioning of a single dominant object – the jug in the shot of fruit here, for example. Other objects should be added one at a time, with frequent checks through the camera's viewfinder to see how the arrangement looks. In the end, you may want to remove some objects because a stark, uncluttered arrangement usually produces the greatest impact.

Johnny Lindo Holland

8

Everyday household objects – perfume bottles, knickknacks, even empty clothes hangers – lend themselves to a still-life composition with a little imagination. This sculptural mobile was suspended and photographed in front of a plain cloth backdrop.

Steve Myers

Lee Howick

A classic still-life arrangement of fruit with a jug becomes unusually tempting because the main lighting comes from an angle above and a dark background brings out the fresh colors. A sprinkling of water increases the sense of lushness.

In a well-planned still life, objects do more than look good together. Here weathered planks suggest that the fish are freshly caught and still on the wharf. And while adding a needed bit of color, the lemon slice signals that the fish will soon appear on a dinner table.

Collectibles

Countless people are collectors. Their stores of treasures range from stamps and coins to beer cans and lightning rod ornaments. Photography can be used for collecting, too, especially of items you cannot simply buy and take home with you.

Signs are among the most popular photographic collectibles because of their diversity and their abundance. With a little diligence, it is fairly easy to build up a photographic collection of signs that have a common theme, whether it be inn signs, billboards, stained glass or neon signs, wall scrawlings, or signs that are simply funny or incongruous.

The list of other photographic collectibles is virtually limitless. Unusual buildings and architectural details – such as windows, doors, or even doorknobs and cornices – readily lend themselves to systematic collection. The same is true of shop windows, especially in antique and junk shops, and of outdoor furnishings, such as ornate street lamps and manhole covers.

Some photographic collectibles, like signs and architectural details, are located above eye level, so it may be useful to have a medium to long telephoto lens (see page 176) that lets you stand back and shoot from an angle that does not distort your subject. A macro lens can also be handy for taking close-ups of details. And if you want to have the features of both lenses in one, a zoom macro lens is a nice compromise, as it allows you to move easily from long views to tight close-ups. For photographs of glass, such as windows, it is helpful to have a polarizing filter to help eliminate reflections (see page 190).

Keith Boas

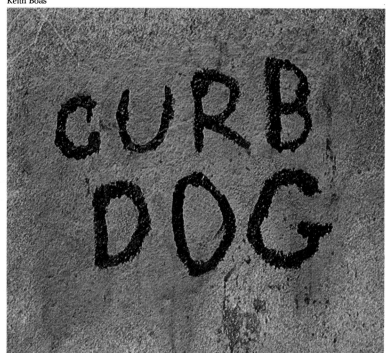

In the irregular formation of the letters, you can almost sense the frustration of the person who painted this injunction to inconsiderate pet owners.

Keith Boas

Careful framing allowed the photographer to transform a common sign into an unexpectedly funny one.

9

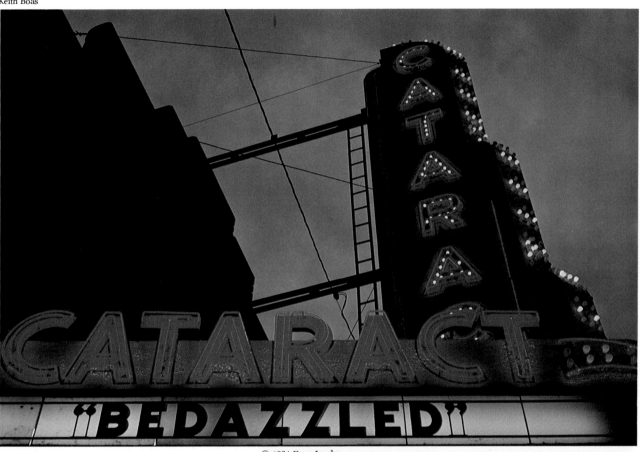

This movie theater in Niagara Falls, New York, brightly displayed its name and feature attraction against a cool-colored evening sky.

Incongruous signs –such as this Venetian blind salesperson's warning to tailgaters –are always fun to collect and fun to show.

Inn signs are a good example of the kind of closely related subjects that can be easily collected in photographs while traveling.

Minor Details

To create some distinctive – and often puzzling – compositions, you can move in so close to your subject that the viewer might not easily recognize the object you have photographed. Rather than merely puzzling, however, close-ups force the viewer to concentrate entirely on visual elements, whether they be shapes, lines, patterns, textures, colors, or any combination of these. Thus, the emphasis of the photograph shifts from a recognizable object to an abstract composition the photographer has created.

Besides being a way to get singular pictures, this approach is good for training your eye. It compels you to take a second, closer look at the parts of a scene. It encourages you to be selective, to use camera angle and the picture's frame to play up visually appealing features. And it prompts you to judge the distances and spatial relationships between objects and their backgrounds and to manipulate depth of field for the effect you want.

Look at the pictures here as studies in pure form. Pay special attention to how color, shapes, and other visual elements interplay. Then turn the page upside down to find out what the photographers used to create their compositions.

Sheldon Berdé

A. A pattern created by repeating areas of black and white becomes a delightful optical puzzle because the viewer loses all sense of its depth.

Roger Abrahams

B. Bursts like flames seem to flare out from the central rectangle and the odd projection below it.

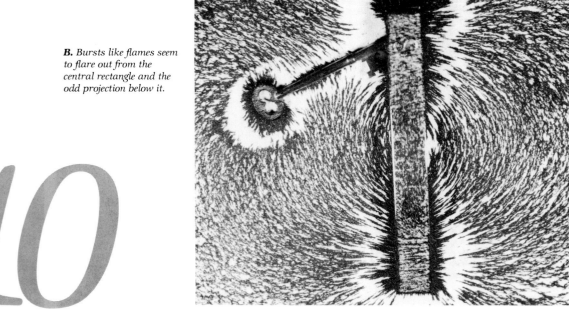

10

Keith Boas

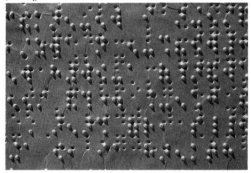

D. *A pattern of bumps and indentations on a copper-colored surface gives this photograph a cool, sculptured quality.*

C. *Converging circles of scalloped lines can create a symmetrical composition with pleasing irregularities.*

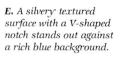

E. *A silvery textured surface with a V-shaped notch stands out against a rich blue background.*

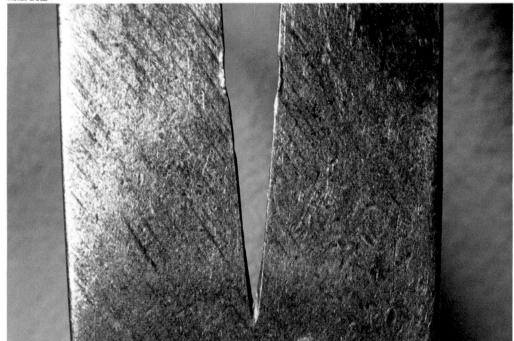

A. Taxis
B. Magnet and shavings
C. Rolled-up carpeting
D. Braille
E. Hammer

People

Good pictures of people attract either the viewer's curiosity or empathy and are always attention-getters. When the subjects are part of a larger scene, as they are in the pictures on these two pages, the photographer has the opportunity to show them interacting with their environments.

In a successful photograph, the relationship between the subjects and their surroundings does two things simultaneously: it deepens our understanding of the subjects and at the same time it creates a visually stimulating composition. Two pictures here by Ernst Haas are excellent examples of this dual accomplishment. The portrait of a woman crossing a street provides a striking study in color contrast as well as a tale of daily chores. And the picture of a father and sons against a wall mural tells of a happy outing and produces the delightful illusion that the subjects are part of the background.

Both posed and candid photographs of people can bear your creative mark. With posed pictures, you have much more control. You can select the setting, lighting, camera angle, and frame that give the best composition, and you can position your subjects carefully within the setting to obtain a special effect. But giving them some degree

Ernst Haas

Jeffrey Sedlick

Lively group portraits of children often end up looking chaotic. In this shot, the photographer circumvented the problem by using the openings in a playground structure to organize and frame the youngsters without inhibiting their natural exuberance.

of freedom can produce a picture with more spontaneity.

With candid pictures, you must respond quickly, and you can gain time to concentrate on composition by having your camera ready. If you use high-speed film outdoors on a fairly bright day, it's easy to take candids. You'll be able to use a small aperture for good depth of field and a fast shutter speed to stop action. A medium telephoto lens is helpful to capture your subjects unaware.

Ernst Haas

A mural painted on a Coney Island refreshment stand allowed Ernst Haas to blend his subjects with the colorful painted characters. The result is a photograph that causes the viewer to look twice.

74 *Special Situations*

Even a person performing a mundane activity can be the subject for an outstanding photograph. Here Ernst Haas captures the strong contrast between a woman's brightly colored dress and her drab surroundings.

11

Faces

Although stance, clothing, and setting can tell an observer quite a bit about a person, the face is undoubtedly the most expressive part of the body. And one of the easiest ways to take an intense and revealing portrait of a person is to concentrate on the face. A tight composition usually conveys a strong feeling of intimacy. This quality is heightened when the subject looks directly into the camera because the viewer of the resulting picture is given the sense of making direct eye contact with the subject.

A close-up of the face also captures fully all the details around the eyes and mouth that reveal the subject's mood and character, producing insightful results. As two of the pictures on these pages show, close-ups are especially effective with children, whose moods and expressions are often unguarded.

The soft, diffused lighting of an overcast day provides flattering illumination for portraits of faces. This light does not produce harsh contrasts between highlighted and shadowed areas, and it prevents subjects from squinting – a common problem in bright sunlight. Used carefully, however, strong directional light can be very dramatic, as shown in the picture of the woman at far right.

If you limit yourself to making head-and-shoulders portraits, a lens with a normal focal length (about 50 mm with a 35 mm camera) can be used without creating too much distortion of the facial features. But you will get a better perspective with a moderately long telephoto lens (100 mm with a 35 mm camera). It lets you move in for tighter compositions that are undistorted, and it lets you keep your distance, which can avoid making your subject feel crowded.

Jeffrey Sedlick

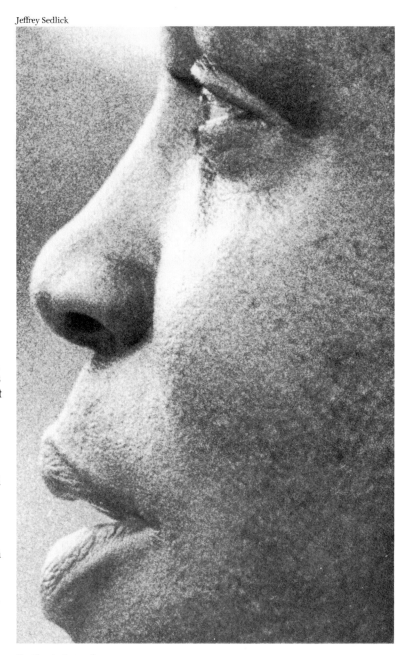

Profile photographs are dramatic, but they are not always as flattering to subjects as this one is.

Brooke Hummer

A bold, unusual pose, a dark background, and strong directional lighting combine to make this portrait starkly dramatic – a quality that is enhanced by the graphic nature of black-and-white photography.

Twinkling eyes and a broad grin convey this young girl's amusement, while a hand to the mouth reveals her shyness.

Daniel Saltzgiver

Mindy Vollmar

The joyful, topsy-turvy world of children at play is captured in the gleeful face of this young rope climber.

Body Features

Selective photographs of people need not be limited to their faces. Isolated segments of the body can also be very expressive. Or they can have sensuous overtones. Even the image of a torso or hands can tell us much about a person's poise or carriage.

To be effective, a photograph of a body feature should be simple and uncluttered. Backgrounds, especially, you should keep uncomplicated – either by using a plain setting as a backdrop or by limiting the lens's depth of field so that the background is indistinct. Flat frontal lighting emphasizes a body part's two-dimensional shape; more angular lighting – preferably from two sources, such as the sun and a reflector – stresses three-dimensional form.

Al Satterwhite/The Image Bank

Any distinctive facial feature can have impact when isolated. For such close-ups, a macro lens or screw-on supplementary close-up lens is needed (see page 182).

Sharon Stirek

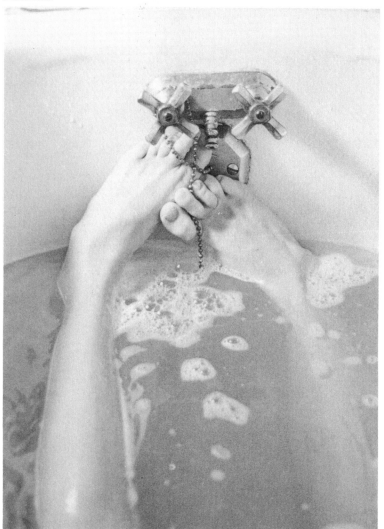

Feet may seem like the most unlikely part of the body to provide an interesting picture, but as this playful bathtub photo shows, an imaginative photographer can make them very expressive.

Brain Frechette

A carefully composed picture of the torsos of two anonymous bathers captures the essence of a day at the beach.

Robert Clemens

A bright blue background provides a strongly contrasting element to set off a simple study of legs.

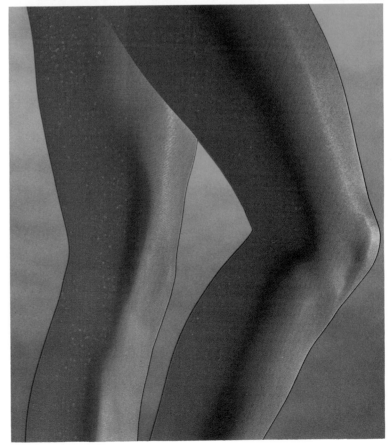

13

Framing

Using a foreground element to create a frame within the picture's frame is one of the oldest tricks in the artist's trade. The framing element not only isolates and emphasizes a subject, but also imparts a feeling of depth. And as an added benefit, it can be used to obscure distracting details or to create an interesting foreground where none exists.

As a compositional technique, framing is often used to turn an otherwise plain scene into a perfectly harmonious one. Some frames, such as an overhanging tree branch or looming rock formation, seem so natural that we aren't even conscious of their presence – just their pleasing effects. But you can also use frames as a creative device, to heighten a picture's impact or offer your viewer a feeling of playfulness.

Frames usually work best when they are thematically related to the subject. In the pictures here, it seems entirely appropriate for the façade of one of thousands of tenements to be framed by a window across the street and for a boy to be framed by a playground tunnel. The shape of a frame is also important. A rectangular frame quietly reinforces the frame of the photograph. Circular, curved, and irregular frames are more dynamic and draw more attention to themselves. Look for unusual frames, too, such as a car door window or a person's outstretched arm. Frames that contrast with the area they surround, either in color or intensity of tone, are most stunning.

Norman Kerr

A pattern of windows in a New York City tenement building is isolated and visually reinforced by being photographed from inside a similar window. Both the frame and the repeating element in the pattern echo one another.

Kim Olsen

A portrait can be much more striking when a handy window, door, or gateway is used as an impromptu frame. Here a young boy is framed by a circular opening in a playground tunnel.

14

Although frames are usually foreground elements, you will sometimes find them at middle distance. The Venetian tunnel here frames both the bow of a gondola approaching it and the scene beyond, creating an illusion of depth.

© 1981 Anthony Edgeworth

A red truck door provides a dramatic frame for a picturesque desert scene and creates an interesting juxtaposition of a brightly colored manufactured object and a more subdued, natural setting.

Low Angles

One way literally to give your pictures a new perspective is to change the vantage point of your camera. Most photographers unnecessarily confine themselves to the normal straight-on point of view that a standing position gives because it is convenient and seems natural. On the other hand, professional photographers have long since discovered that when a subject or composition lacks visual drama, one of the easiest ways of achieving it is to shift the point of view of the camera. Depending on the subject, they may decide to shoot from a lower, upward-looking vantage point, as in these pictures. Or they may seek a higher point of view, as shown on pages 84 and 85. Each has very different advantages.

   With a large subject, such as a tall building or monument, you can achieve a low point of view by simply moving close to the subject and pointing the camera upward. With subjects that are closer to the ground, you may have to squat or lie down to obtain a low vantage point. But in either case the effects are similar. The subject immediately gains in stature, often becoming a looming presence against a backdrop of sky, trees, or ceiling. This stature is all the more evident because directing the camera upward usually eliminates distracting foreground details. Even with a commonplace subject, such as the beach chairs at far right, the results can be startling because the normal sense of scale is reversed and unexpected lines and patterns are revealed. This effect can be enhanced by using a wide-angle lens.

   With rectangular subjects, a low angle often produces a form of image distortion known as keystoning, which occurs because the film plane is not parallel to the subject. Typically, the sides of a tall building shot with an upward-angled camera become rapidly converging lines in the upper part of the picture. Keystoning can be deliberately exaggerated to produce a special effect. It can be used to make a building look taller or to distort everyday objects, such as the cases of mineral water shown here. Keystoning is not limited to low angles. From a high angle, keystoning can produce a picture of a person with a large head and tiny feet. Used horizontally, it can make a fence or wall seem to extend endlessly into the distance.

The dramatic effect of keystoning can be seen in this picture of Perrier crates. The lines and words quickly converge toward the upper part of the image, creating the impression that the crates extend ceaselessly upward.

An upward-angled shot of the Statue of Liberty provides a fresh perspective on a familiar landmark and underscores its massive size.

Paul Freedman

Jack Zehrt

Shooting from a low angle, the photographer used the foreground figure of a relaxing bather as a partial frame for a diver frozen at the height of a back dive.

Marvin Lyons/The Image Bank

15

A worm's eye view of beach chairs causes them to loom like monumental structures, emphasizing the strong angular lines of the frames and the linear pattern of the webbing.

At the same time, the chairs form a frame for the distant couple.

High Angles

Pointing your camera down on a subject produces the opposite effect of assuming a low point of view. Rather than exaggerating the size and importance of the subject, a high angle tends to lessen the individual significance of the subject and shows it as part of a pattern. In other words, a high angle literally gives an overview, as is shown here in the pictures of the vegetable stand and the man with an umbrella.

A high angle can also eliminate a cluttered background and replace it with a flat expanse of lawn, sand, or pavement. In addition, it can help you fool the viewer, as in the picture immediately at the right. Had it been taken straight on, you would more easily recognize its true subject – department store mannequins and window dressing props!

Stairways, escalators, windows on upper floors, observation platforms, bridges, and ski lifts provide some ready-made high vantage points. Good subjects include auto and pedestrian traffic patterns, boats and their wakes, some sporting events, and patterns in sand and snow. If you are flying in an aircraft, watch for interesting patterns on the ground, such as cars in a parking lot, the S curve in a river, rows of trees and planted fields, and ribbons of highways winding over the landscape.

For a portable high-angle platform, consider the flexibility of ladders. You can move them around, as well as move up and down on them. When going into the field, many professional photographers build a platform on the roof of their car by attaching a couple of cross supports to the luggage rack and topping it with a sturdy sheet of plywood.

George Weber

Photographed from over one mannequin's shoulder, this intriguing view of gloves, shoes, and accessories suggests preparations for a formal occasion.

From the vantage point of an upper-story window, the snow-covered umbrella of a passerby is pleasingly juxtaposed with a trio of trash can lids.

A basket of bright red peppers nestled among an array of predominantly green vegetables at a produce stand becomes a harmonious still life when photographed from directly above.

The Power of Color

Any picture that promotes color from its usual supporting role to a center-stage position immediately becomes visually compelling. Learning how to emphasize color is mainly a matter of training your eye to recognize situations in which color predominates – of selecting and minimizing the number of colors in a scene or of isolating a colorful element. When it comes to doing this, Pete Turner is widely acknowledged as a master. In his photograph of a Greek church in simulated moonlight, all the colors are closely related hues of blue and violet, and the photograph's impact comes from the overall harmony of these hues. Other pictures may derive their impact from the contrast between a colorful detail and a muted background, and sometimes all that is needed is a splash of a very bright color or two.

In some pictures, the key to an effective color shot is in how the camera is positioned to frame the scene. It can be angled to show the relationship between some colors and to exclude others. Or it can be moved to isolate dominant colors against a neutral background. In other pictures, the pervasive color may come from the quality of the light. This is especially true at night, early or late in the day, and with certain types of artificial light.

In selecting colors, don't overlook their psychological impact. We tend to think of colors from one side of the spectrum – red, orange, and yellow – as being warm and exciting. They assert themselves in a picture, and objects in the colors seem to be larger and heavier than they actually are. Colors from the other side of the spectrum – green, blue, indigo, and violet – are generally thought of as being cool and calming. They seem to recede and make an object look smaller and lighter in weight.

17

Pete Turner/The Image Bank

Harmony results when most of the hues in a scene are closely related. A predominance of blues, introduced by a filter in this photograph by Pete Turner, simulates moonlight and conveys a feeling of serenity. The church is located on the Greek island of Mikonos.

Marcella S. Martin

Colors stand out most vividly against a dark background. Here the woman's black dress and the shadowy area behind her form a strong frame for her multicolored bouquet of paper flowers.

▶

Pete Turner created this famous color composition by careful selection of camera angle. By lining up the top of the trash barrel with the horizon, he fashioned a geometric arrangement that sets off the bright container against the white beach and balances its reds and yellows with the expanse of deep blue sky above.

Pete Turner/The Image Bank

Contrasting Colors

Contrast between colors in a photograph can yield unexpectedly rewarding results. But these results can differ greatly, depending on whether the contrast is bold or subtle. If the contrast is between two or more equally strong colors, as in Pete Turner's close-up of the umbrella below, the impact comes from colors competing for the eye's attention. Instead of drawing the eye into the picture to convey a sense of depth, the contrast tends to keep it surface-bound, making the image seem flatter. As a result, the subject is perceived more as a pattern or design. Such contrasts are usually most forceful with subjects that present a strong formal arrangement.

A bold yet balanced contrast is set up when brightly colored subjects are played off a solid background color, as in Ernst Haas's group portrait at far right. The contrast here causes the subjects to stand out from the setting and draws the eye into the group of peasant women, lending depth and personality to otherwise anonymous subjects.

Contrasts in color, however, need not be dramatic to be effective. As illustrated in the picture of the Indian woman in a sari, even a subdued hue can be eye-catching if it is set off by a soft complementary-toned background.

Ric Ergenbright

In this picture taken in India, the subtle contrast between the woman's blue sari and the ivory-toned colonnade is heightened because she is the only element disrupting a strong geometric pattern.

Pete Turner/The Image Bank

A bold clash between two dominant colors turns Pete Turner's close-up of a beach umbrella into a semi-abstract design.

18

Ernst Haas

A multitude of bright colors in a pleasing circular pattern adds motion and depth to this German group study by one of the masters of color photography, Ernst Haas.

Black-and-White Contrast

In black-and-white photography, the colors in a scene are translated into black, white, and the many shades of grey in between. Most scenes contain a large range of these tonal gradations. However, if you limit the tones in a picture to the darkest and lightest ones, a great deal of strength and drama can be created. Sometimes a scene itself offers strong contrasts, as in the picture at far right of a dark figure walking through a snow-covered park. Contrast also can be created, however, by careful selection of lighting and camera angle.

Hard, direct lighting usually produces the greatest contrast by highlighting some areas while casting others into deep shadows. Backlighting of any sort, even from a soft, diffused source, also creates strong contrasts by darkly silhouetting the subject against a light background, as in the two pictures on this page of the fire escape and a person's shoulder.

The photograph of the fire escape is also a good example of how your camera angle can increase contrast. On a grey day, the photographer aimed the camera straight upward, removing all other detail from the scene. No matter what method you use to achieve it, high contrast is most effective with strong, simple compositions in which lines and shapes prevail.

Keith Boas

An upward view isolating a fire escape against the sky creates a boldly contrasting pattern of lines. The angled position of the subject heightens the picture's dynamism.

Gabrielle Perdrizet

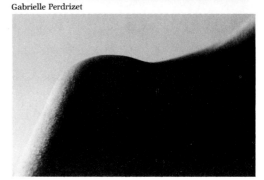

Lighted along only its outer edge, the shoulder of a dark figure becomes a dramatic study in shape because of the strong contrast in tones.

Sidney Hecker

In this picture of a solitary stroller in New York City's Central Park, a high camera angle allowed the photographer to isolate the dark elements against the snow, heightening the contrast.

Muted Colors

Bright, vibrant colors may be the most immediately striking, but there are many scenes that appeal to the eye because their colors are understated. A preponderance of subdued colors in a picture creates a restful and harmonious mood. Unlike strong colors, which compete with each other or overwhelm less prominent hues in the scene, muted colors – soft pastels, faded primary colors, or nature's hues – offer a delicate interplay that allows the viewer to appreciate subtler differences.

Many subjects have colors that are naturally muted, such as the eucalyptus tree bark in the picture here. Other subjects appear to have subdued colors because of the quality of the light. The faint light of dawn or dusk or of a heavily overcast day makes all colors less assertive. Exposure also affects color intensity. Hues are less saturated when you slightly overexpose color slide film or slightly underexpose color negative film by adjusting your aperture. To overexpose, use a half-stop larger aperture than your meter dictates; to underexpose, use a half-stop smaller aperture. On an automatic camera, temporarily reset your film-speed dial one ASA setting lower for overexposure and one setting higher for underexposure.

Russell Lamb

In this close-up of a eucalyptus tree, the contrast between two equally understated hues, pale green and tan, creates a subtle nature study.

Ric Ergenbright

In a picture in which very subdued hues predominate, a bit of bright color, such as the red rim of the boat here, can emphasize rather than destroy the prevailing mood.

Neil Montanus

The faded but still festive colors of Brazilian houses provide a background that is distinctive yet does not distract from the human subject. The deliberate blurring of the boy and the ball creates the impression of motion (see page 154).

Ken Ferrell

Muted colors can be found in all kinds of weather conditions, even on a relatively clear, sunny day. Here the grey trunk, snow-blown branches, and ground foliage join the blue sky in creating a harmonious blend of muted pastels.

20

High Key

One very effective way of creating mood in a photograph is to control the lightness or darkness of the tones. In high-key pictures, such as the ones shown here, light and medium tones predominate. The mood they convey is one of airiness and delicacy, softness and spaciousness.

In creating a high-key picture, your choice of subject matter is crucial. Generally, both the main subject and the background should be light in tone, such as a white horse against sand or a light-haired model bathed in sunlight from an open window or door. It is not essential that every part of the scene be completely light toned, however. A small area of darkness can point up the prevalent lightness of the image by contrast, as the ballet dancer's leotard does in the scene at right.

For a successful high-key picture, the lighting should be diffused and even, producing a minimum of dark, shadowed areas. You can heighten the dreamy atmosphere of a high-key picture by strong backlighting, provided the exposure on your camera is set for the important parts of the scene. Such an exposure will turn the backlighting into a diffused, overexposed area, like the windows in the dance studio. A high-key effect is also increased by any factor that causes light to spread and diffuse, such as fog or mist (see page 114) and soft-focus attachments (see page 186).

A high-key photograph must be exposed with care. The light meter on a camera is designed to respond to a scene with an average range of tones. A scene with only light tones will make the camera indicate a smaller aperture or a faster shutter speed than is actually needed, resulting in an underexposed image. A solution is to use an 18 percent grey card to determine exposure (see page 34). Some, but by no means all, high-key photographs benefit from increasing the exposure from a grey-card reading to create an overexposure. Experiment by making two or three exposures with different settings. If you are using an automatic camera, you should compensate for the effect of the light tones by adjusting the meter (see page 36).

Duncan Thorn

P. J. Crerar

A hazy atmosphere and soft lighting reinforce the high-key effect created by the light and medium tones of grey here. The effect gives this industrial complex an ethereal, futuristic appearance.

Donald Maggio

Overexposure and a soft-focus lens (see page 186) combined to create this delicate high-key mood. Had the exposure been normal, the heavily overcast sky would have been recorded as a dull grey instead of a solid wash of white.

Light pouring through the windows increases the airy openness of a dance studio. With such backlighting, however, it is important to set your exposure for the main subject and allow the bright backlighting to become overexposed and diffused.

Low Key

When a person is described as low key, we imagine someone who is restrained and unexciting. But a good low-key picture, consisting primarily of dark tones, conveys a mood that is somber and often mysterious. The picture's drama usually comes from highlighted elements – the distinctive shape of a hat, a bicycle, or a river appearing out of moody shadows – that stand out in bold counterpoint to the prevalent darkness.

Selecting subject matter with the right amount of contrast is of utmost importance in taking a low-key picture. By squinting as you view a scene, you can previsualize the result. A common problem in exposing a low-key scene is having insufficient light to activate the camera's meter. If your camera can be used in manual mode, one way to get a reading in dim light is to divide your film's ISO/ASA rating by five. Set the resulting number (or the number nearest to it) on your ASA dial. Then take a reading off a sheet of plain white paper. For example, if you are using 400-speed film, set 80 (one-fifth of 400) on your ASA dial and

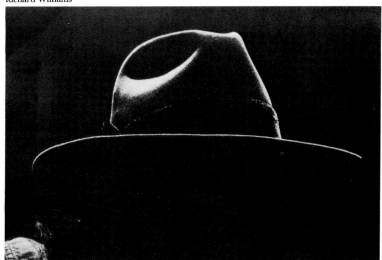

Richard Williams

take a reading off a white surface. Be sure to switch the ASA dial back to its normal setting before taking other pictures.

After getting a reading this way, you may want to try additional exposures at one or two f-stops smaller. If the highlighted areas in the picture are bright enough, such underexposure can deepen and darken shadowy areas, heightening the contrast.

Light from almost directly overhead delineates the distinctive creased crown and wide brim of a fedora, while casting a deep shadow over the face.

Chris Campbell

In a shadowy basement, light filtering through a stairwell outlines the shape of a bicycle, creating a classic low-key still life.

David Sumner

A touch of color can greatly enhance the dramatic effect of a low-key photograph. Here a band of dark blue, cloud-dappled sky provides an unexpected backdrop for a majestic view of Washington State's Flaming Gorge River as it snakes its way through a dark valley.

22

Early and Late in the Day

The light available at different times of the day greatly affects the mood and atmosphere of a photograph. And the light is especially dramatic during two brief periods – the half-hour or so after sunrise and the half-hour or so before sunset. When the sun is low in the sky, its light rakes across the landscape, creating long shadows that bring out textures. And sometimes shapes are emphatically defined by crisp contrasts between shadows and highlights.

Because sunlight cuts through the atmosphere at a long, low angle, many of its wavelengths from the blue-violet end of the spectrum are scattered and absorbed by the air, and the light that reaches us has an abundance of flattering warm yellows, oranges, and reds. Blues may not be entirely absent, however. Areas of the sky away from the sun may be intensely blue, as in the picture of houses here. And shaded areas of snow, frost, or sand may reflect the color of the sky, as in the photograph of a snowy landscape at far right.

Although larger vistas usually benefit from the particular qualities of early morning or late afternoon light, this illumination can also give warmth and intimacy to a portrait, as in the photograph below of a young woman with her guitar. Other creative effects that can be achieved when the sun is low in early morning and late afternoon are shown on the following pages.

Charles Newman

Lighted frontally by a sun low in the sky, a row of beach houses takes on a warm tint that contrasts dramatically with the rich blue sky behind them. The lighting seems to give the houses the unreal appearance of carefully executed models.

Kodak Pathé

In some portraits, the warm hues of late afternoon light can be very flattering, giving the skin a healthy, ruddy glow. In this case, they also complement the red of the young French woman's dress and the blonde wood of her guitar.

23

David Sumner

Although the first light of morning has asserted itself in the background, night still persists in the long shadows on the western slope of a Utah mountain. The tiny pair of headlights in the lower right-hand corner confirms the presence of dawn and adds compositional interest to the picture.

Rim Lighting

When a strong light source, such as the early morning or late afternoon sun, is directly behind a subject, it can produce a brilliant rim of light that seems to emanate from within the subject. The effect is most pronounced along edges that catch the light and diffuse it, such as hair and sheer clothing, the fine filaments and drops of liquid on a leaf, or the translucent edge of a dark cloud.

In portraits, the atmosphere of luminosity that rim lighting creates can be very flattering, particularly when the subject's hair has an interesting texture. In shooting, though, you must use extra care to prevent the subject from being turned into a dark silhouette by the strong backlighting. The front of the subject should be lighted from a soft, diffused light source, such as a reflector or a white wall. And you must expose for the relatively dim illumination on the subject.

With a camera that can be used in manual mode, take a light reading by angling the camera so that the lens receives light from only the subject. With an automatic camera that has an exposure adjustment switch, set it for one or two *f*-stops more exposure. For completely automatic cameras that have no exposure override control, reset the camera's ASA dial to half of your film's normal rating to get one stop more exposure (see page 36). The extra effort will be worth it. The bright background will become very overexposed, heightening the luminous atmosphere.

For certain subjects, such as the leaves shown here, you may want to create the effect of silhouetting to delineate the shapes dramatically. In this case, you should experiment by underexposing the subject one or two *f*-stops.

As a dark thunderhead passes in front of the sun, the cloud's leading edge is dramatically outlined in white.

Michael Sutton

Backlighting that catches on filaments and dewdrops sharply defines the shapes of leaves and at the same time silhouettes them, creating a dark picture with mysterious overtones.

▶ *A young girl takes on an almost angelic glow as strong sunlight brilliantly halos her hair and gives a soft translucence to her gown.*

Gene Ursch

Shadows

The long shadows created in early morning and late afternoon are so pronounced and dramatic that they themselves can become subjects for photographs. Shadows cast by people, especially, can be intriguing. They are expressive and familiar, and yet they are also anonymous because the figure casting the shadow could be anyone.

The moods shadows convey can be quietly evocative, perhaps even ominous, as in the picture at far right below of the man's shadow in an entryway. Or they can be playful, like the children's shadows with chalked-in smiles. Long shadows cast by any object or a myriad of shadows can also become an integral part of a picture's design, as the two pictures on this page show.

Shadows are most effective when they contrast with a light-colored background. They can be darkened by slightly underexposing the scene a half or full stop. With an automatic camera you will need to use your film-speed dial to compensate. Temporarily reset the dial at one or two ASA stops higher. Be sure to return it to its regular setting when you move on to other subjects.

David Sumner

Long afternoon shadows link a random growth of daisies into a striking and effective pattern.

Sunlight streaming through a beamed skylight creates a myriad of strong diagonal shadows. The intricacy of the floor tiles plays against the crisscross effect of the shadows and darkened recesses.

Jonathan Chow

Chris Lombardo

For this whimsical group portrait, the photographer lined up five young models and chalked in smiling faces on their shadows. The final picture was turned upside down to make the joke complete.

Gary Weinreb

Late afternoon sunlight streaming into a hallway has been interrupted by an unseen form whose presence is revealed – somewhat disturbingly – by his shadow.

25

Silhouettes

When a subject is strongly backlighted, the usual rule in photography is to set the exposure for the subject and let the background become overexposed and washed out. But in some situations you might want to reverse this dictum. The effect is especially interesting when simple, distinctive subjects stand out as totally dark silhouettes against a brightly colored natural background, looking almost as if they had been cut out and superimposed. The eye of the viewer is immediately drawn to the subject by the unexpected juxtaposition.

Since the background is important in a silhouette picture, the backlighting that produces the silhouette should not come from a direct source of light unless it is diffused by a translucent screen, as in the photograph at far right below. Instead, look for situations in which light reflects off the background. Water, the sky, and light-colored buildings and cliffs are good sources of reflected light. If the subject takes up only a small part of the scene and is much darker in tone than the background, a normal exposure will usually yield a strong silhouette on film. If the background is closer in tone to the subject, a slight underexposure (see page 36) will help intensify the silhouette.

Kodak Pathé

The striking contrast between the curving, fluid forms of a statue and the sharp rectilinear design of a skyscraper was heightened by silhouetting the statue.

Twilight is always a good time for silhouettes. But for figures to stand out, they must be isolated against a lighter area, such as the shiny surface of the water in this picture of boatmen on a river in India.

Ric Ergenbright

David William Hamilton

In this photograph by David Hamilton, the silhouette of an elk stands proudly amidst a landscape of intensely rich hues.

A hot air balloon provides a gigantic translucent backdrop that silhouettes the figures of its crew. In silhouette, the shapes of people can be revealing, especially if they are caught, as here, in profile.

Martin Folb

26

Sunrise, Sunset

Lee Howick

Sunrise and sunset are two of nature's grandest spectacles. Whether they are the main subject of a picture or are included in a broader vista, they assure an image with a dramatically heightened mood. Fortunately, both sunrises and sunsets can be recorded successfully on film over a wide range of exposure settings, allowing you to determine the effect that is best for a particular scene. As an extremely bright source of light, however, the sun will cause your camera's built-in meter to respond inaccurately when it is included in the scene.

If the sun itself is the subject of your picture, take your reading from the brightness of the sky and clouds – not directly from the sun. This will slightly underexpose the scene and produce deep rich colors in the clouds. It will also darken the foreground so that trees, buildings, or people will be silhouetted against the sky, forming a dramatic frame. The effect can be heightened by giving a scene an *f*-stop or two less exposure, as in the photograph of an African plain at lower right. Look especially for scenes with a slight amount of haze or mist, as the fine particles of water in the air will pick up and reflect the sun's colors. And try using a telephoto lens to make the sun appear larger and more dominant.

If the sun is to be a backdrop for a more panoramic picture, angle your camera downward and take a reading off the foreground. This will prevent the foreground from becoming a silhouette, but the sun and sky will be overexposed, appearing lighter and closer to normal daylight. Similarly, you can often get more dramatic results by shooting when the sun is not in the picture – when it is hidden behind a cloud or at the moment just after it sets or just before it rises.

Ric Ergenbright

The sun becomes a massive ball of fire as it sets behind Africa's famous Serengeti plain. A mist faintly silhouettes a line of zebras in the foreground.

A calm prevails as the sun sets over Hong Kong's usually bustling harbor. The sun's position behind a cloud made the sky's colors deeper and richer, and the body of water enhances the scene by reflecting the sky's colors.

Colour Library International

The colors of a sunrise or sunset can vary greatly from place to place, and from moment to moment in the same place. In this Japanese sunrise, unusual lavender hues create a delicate, contemplative mood.

Dawn and Dusk

For a half-hour or so before the sun rises and after it sets, the sky is filled with a soft, rapidly changing light that has an almost magical ability to transform scenes. Starting with the first faint light at daybreak, colors brighten by the minute, going from cool blues through an ever-shifting series of pearly pastels to the warm hues that immediately precede sunrise. Forms that are, at first, merged into one shadowy shape gradually and almost imperceptibly become distinct and identifiable. In the evening after the sun stages its dramatic exit, the process is repeated in reverse.

To take advantage of these twilight periods, it's best to be prepared. Because the light changes so quickly, scout a scene in advance for the best camera angle. And because the light is so dim, plan to use a high-speed film.

A tripod or other firm camera support is also advisable. You might want to use a fairly small aperture to get good depth of field, which will often require exposure times too long for hand holding the camera. A photo of a skyline taken about 10 minutes after sunset might require a setting of 1/60 second at $f/8$ with 400-speed film, allowing the camera to be hand held. But by a half-hour after sunset, you'll probably need a full second at $f/8$, and that scene can only be taken with the camera on a support.

Check exposure readings frequently; the darker the scene, the more important it is to bracket your exposure a full stop or more in either direction. If you have an automatic camera, bracket by temporarily changing the film-speed dial setting to half and then double the correct setting. This not only gives you an acceptable picture, but also allows you to select the final image nearest to the actual effect you want.

Twilight is also the time to take pictures that give the illusion of night. You should take these photgraphs during the few short minutes when the sky is deep blue, just after the darkness of night vanishes in the morning and just before it returns in the evening. The faint light still in the sky silhouettes subjects on the horizon while street lamps and other lights convey the impression of night.

George Elich

A pine bough forms a dramatic frame for the deep ruddy glow of late twilight and for the figure of a boy silhouetted against the reflected sky.

Kathleen Norris Cook

A blanket of snow in
Arizona's high country
reflects the cold blue of
a cloudy dawn. An
informal arrangement of
pine trees provides a
foreground frame of
restful silhouettes for the
approaching sunrise.

John Henkel

Dawn over Florence,
Italy, finds silhouetted
bridges mirrored
perfectly in the placid
waters of the Arno River.
Pictures taken at dawn
nearly always convey a
sense of peace because of
the absence of activity.

Moonlight

We have a lot of associations with moonlight–romance, mystery, peacefulness– and it is relatively easy to record those moods on film. A scene illuminated by moonlight, however, is about two million times (21 f-stops) dimmer than one illuminated by direct sunlight. So in order to get a good image, plan to shoot on nights when the sky is relatively clear and the moon is full or close to it. Also use a tripod or other firm camera support so that you can take long exposures. And use a high-speed film, possibly one that you can have push-processed for a higher ASA rating (see page 49).

To get correct exposure, use the exposure table below or a very sensitive meter. The danger in using a meter is, surprisingly, that you may overexpose the scene. The meter is programmed to indicate settings that will make the scene appear of average brightness. By following the meter exactly, it is easy to make a moonlit scene look as if it had been taken in daylight. To avoid this result, use 25 to 50 percent less exposure than your meter indicates. On an automatic camera, set the exposure override control in the underexposure direction or reset your film-speed dial to twice its correct setting. This exposure adjustment is essential with slide films. It is less critical with negative films because the lightness or darkness of the image can be controlled during the printmaking process.

The type of film you select can also have a major effect on the color in the final image of a moonlit scene. A film balanced for tungsten light will produce a cool blue cast, as in the picture at right below of the snowbound house. A daylight-balanced slide film or a color negative film will favor the red end of the spectrum and give the picture a warmer appearance, as in the photograph of the tree immediately at right.

Moonlit Landscapes

ISO/ASA	EXPOSURE
64–100	30 seconds at $f/2$
125–200	15 seconds at $f/2$
250–400	8 seconds at $f/2$
800	4 seconds at $f/2$

Lorna Humes

On nights when the moon is less than full, tones are dim and most details are difficult or impossible to see. Taking advantage of the faint glow in a post-twilight western sky, the photographer partially silhouetted this majestic tree with an exposure of 5 minutes at f/2.8.

An enormous full moon peeking over a mountain in the background adds a great deal of drama to this night shot of a harbor. The moon can be made to look larger by using a telephoto lens, which will also make background elements, like the mountain, appear closer (see page 176).

In this peaceful moonlit snowscape, the prevalence of blue intensifies the feeling of coldness and the snug isolation of the house. Using a tungsten-balanced film (see page 46) heightens the blueness of a moonlit scene.

Overcast Days

On dank, dreary days when the sky is grey and the light is flat, most photographers are inclined to leave their cameras at home. But the potential for creative picture taking is actually much greater on an overcast day than on one dominated by a bright, cheery sun. The chief reason is the quality of the light.

Rather than producing harsh contrasts between bright highlights and deep shadows, light filtered through a canopy of clouds is even and diffused. Contrasts are soft and subtle. Colors are rich and fully saturated. Bright colors that would ordinarily clash with each other or overwhelm muted hues become more harmonious and part of a unified image, as in the picture of the boatyard here.

Scenes photographed on an overcast day usually work best when you move in close and fill the entire image area with shapes and colors, since the sky is often an uninteresting, washed-out grey or white. Sometimes, however, a bland sky can provide a plain backdrop that sharply sets off interesting foreground elements. But as the picture of a park bench at far right shows, try to keep your horizon line relatively high so that there is more ground than sky, and, if possible, mask part of the sky with a foreground frame such as overhanging tree branches.

Even when the sky looks grey, it can still be bright, and when it is included in a scene, it can mislead your camera's meter into making an underexposure that silhouettes the foreground. Take your reading off the foreground or an 18 percent grey card.

The lighting on an overcast day is excellent for outdoor portraits. Its soft, diffused quality is always flattering because it gently reveals the contours of the face with faint, almost imperceptible shadows.

David William Hamilton

David Hamilton, a photographer noted for his evocative images, used the soft quality of overcast lighting to obtain this impressionistic rendering.

David William Hamilton

In a Brazilian boatyard, the contrast between subtle rust stains and brightly painted bows is reduced by diffused overcast lighting.

Chun Brown

When an overcast sky is included in a picture, it usually reproduces as an overexposed, washed-out white. In this photo, it was used to advantage to provide a clean, uncluttered backdrop for the tree and bench.

Scattered puddles on the ground create a broken reflection of the tree trunk and its long branch. For accurate exposure, the light reading was taken off the ground, which offered a good midtone.

Robert Laster

The soft, even lighting on overcast days contributes significantly to the naturalness of portraits. Not only is the light itself flattering, but subjects don't squint and are less inclined to assume a stiff pose.

Special Situations **113**

Fog and Mist

The soft, hazy atmosphere created by fog and mist can be especially effective in photographs because it obscures more than it shows. In fog or mist, the farther an object is from the camera, the more it seems to dissolve and merge with the murky background. Even a fairly cluttered scene, such as a forest, is greatly simplified. Only subjects close to your camera stand out, and colors are so muted that they look almost monochromatic.

Fog, like sand and snow, is a bright, high-key subject and can fool a light meter into calling for underexposure. The best exposure will frequently be one to two f-stops more exposure than what the meter says. It's usually best to take the meter reading off an 18 percent grey card or a middle tone in the foreground.

Carol Simowitz

© 1981 Bill Carter

A tower of San Francisco's Golden Gate Bridge looks as if it is floating in clouds as it projects above a pea-soup sea fog.

The impression of a father and son enjoying a shared pastime is conveyed by these figures silhouetted against a morning mist.

The best place to find hazy conditions is on or near bodies of water, and the best time of day is early morning, before the sun has had a chance to burn off the night's accumulation of mist. Look for strong, distinctive shapes, especially ones that stand out against the haziness as dark silhouettes. Because the lighting is usually dim, plan to use a high-speed film and, if you go out especially early, take along a tripod for the necessary long exposures.

31

▶

A white hat and shoes draw attention to the stroller in a fog-bound forest. The trees in this scene provide a good example of atmospheric perspective – the feeling of distance that is imparted when haze in the air makes objects look fainter in tone as they recede.

Jerry Shubert

Storms and Lightning

Storms, especially electrical storms, are among the most spectacular shows staged by nature, and capturing them on film is challenging. Luckily, the most dramatic shots of storm clouds can be taken as the storm approaches or leaves. As the photograph at right shows, it is during these transitional periods that you get striking contrasts between areas that are clouded and ones that are sunlit. Sunlight breaking through dark clouds or creating bright rim lighting along their edges is especially attractive. Since lighting conditions are uneven and rapidly changing at such times, be sure to bracket your exposures.

Lightning can usually be photographed only during the height of a storm. To protect both yourself and your camera, you should always take your pictures from a safe cover. It is next to impossible to photograph lightning during the daytime unless you are waiting with eye on the viewfinder and finger on the shutter. And even then you may just miss it. You'll find it much easier to work and will usually get more dramatic results if you make a time exposure at night.

Set up your camera on a tripod and point it at the area of the sky where most of the lightning seems to be occurring. Set your camera's shutter speed dial on B. Then open the shutter using a cable release and hold it open until a bolt streaks out of the clouds. Be sure to work in a dark area and to pick a scene that does not include light from houses or street lights. Exposure is mostly a matter of guesswork. Bracket by making several time exposures at different apertures. A good starting point is $f/5.6$ with ISO/ASA 64 film. Holding the shutter open for too long causes an overexposure of the surrounding area. Heat flashes between clouds can also ruin a frame.

Capturing a series of flashes in a scene with light sources, like the skyline at far right, is even trickier. Generally, you will want to use a smaller aperture and a slower speed film so that you can keep the shutter open longer.

A boat and its passengers look almost insignificant beneath the majestic canopy provided by a storm front.

32

Ray Atkeson

In a spectacular display, forked lightning dances menacingly in gloomy skies over Denver. A long exposure on slow-speed film is usually needed to record a multiple series of flashes.

William Quinn

A touch of luck and a preset camera were needed to get this shot of lightning appearing to strike a car during a thunderstorm.

Rainbows

In the aftermath of a rainstorm, nature sometimes provides us with one of its most delicate visual treats, the rainbow. A rainbow is caused by particles of moisture in the air that act as tiny prisms to diffract the light, breaking it up into a spectral array of wavelengths of different colors. The phenomenon is not limited to rain-soaked skies; it can occur any place where there is an abundance of moisture in the air. A waterfall, a public fountain, or even a morning mist will often sport a miniature rainbow when sunlight hits at the proper angle.

Rainbows are very transient, rarely lasting more than a few minutes. When you spot one, you have to act quickly. In composing your picture, the chief problem is usually trying to locate, on such short notice, foreground elements that will add interest to the scene. A rainbow alone is beautiful but not likely to be visually compelling. A foreground, such as sailboats, icy branches, or stone figures, provides a sense of place and completes the composition. In exposure, a problem can occur if a large expanse of relatively bright sky is included in the scene. In this case, it is best to take a reading off the foreground. Or, if you want to produce a greater saturation of colors in the rainbow, try underexposing one half-stop from the reading you derived from the foreground. On an automatic camera, temporarily reset your film-speed dial one ASA setting higher.

Carol Simowitz

A slate-grey sky provides a dark background, setting off this particularly rich-colored rainbow.

33

Lloyd Englert

An ice-encrusted embankment creates a pleasing foreground for a brilliant rainbow formed by mist over water.

A rainbow forms an unexpected but appropriate frame for a row of ancient stone monuments on Easter Island. The age and meaning of these intriguing statues remain a mystery.

Ric Ergenbright

Fireworks

At night a wide variety of light sources can provide subjects for creative photographs, and fireworks are among the most spectacular. But as you will see on the following pages, you can also obtain dramatic results with stars, illuminated signs, vehicle lights, and even ordinary lights on buildings.

   With today's high-speed films, many of the brighter of these light sources can be photographed at shutter speeds that allow you to hand hold the camera. Other sources may require longer exposures, either because the lights are dim or because a long exposure is needed to achieve a special effect. For such time exposures, you need a sturdy tripod or some other firm camera support. Also, have a cable release with a locking mechanism that allows you to keep the shutter open without having to keep your hand on the shutter release and risk movement. Another handy item to have along is a watch that indicates seconds, and when working at night, it is useful to have a small flashlight for making camera settings, reading your watch, and taking notes.

   Fireworks usually require a few seconds of exposure to record the full impact of a burst. Both the initial explosion and the light trails created when burning particles begin to fall are sensational. A single burst looks best when it fills the entire image area. And unless you are close to the fireworks, you will usually need a telephoto lens. To expose for a single burst, set your camera's shutter speed dial on B. Use $f/8$ for a 64-speed film. Press the shutter button just as the explosion begins, and release it when the burst starts to fade. If the scene is fairly dark with no other strong light sources, exposure is not too critical. A larger lens opening, such as $f/5.6$, will make the lines in the burst thicker and lighter, whereas a smaller opening, such as $f/11$, will make them thinner and darker.

   From a distant vantage point with a normal or wide-angle lens, you will get the most spectacular results when you shoot a series of bursts, recording them one after the other on the same frame of film. With the use of a cable release, one easy way to obtain multiple bursts is to lock your camera's shutter on B for the entire series and to put a lens cap on the camera between bursts. If the bursts are going off fairly rapidly, you

Spencer Blank/FPG

Robert Fish

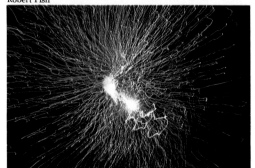

can just hold your hand or a piece of cardboard close to the lens in between bursts. With some cameras, you can also take multiple exposures on the same frame by pressing in the film rewind release button as you move the film advance lever. With both methods, you have to be careful not to disturb the camera, especially if you want to avoid blurring a stationary element, such as a skyline. Or you can deliberately jiggle the camera during the exposures to achieve an effect like the one shown above.

When photographing fireworks, exposure is not too critical, although a setting of f/8 is generally considered best with a 64-speed film.

Like the picture at right, this fireworks photograph is a multiple exposure. The difference is that the photographer deliberately jiggled the camera during each exposure to create jagged light trails.

▶

Capturing one full burst, along with other partial and fading bursts, in a tightly cropped picture conveys the festive, yet ephemeral, nature of fireworks.

34

Barbara Adams/FPG

Neon Lights

Neon tubes are a unique and highly photogenic light source. Rather than producing a bright concentration of light, they emit a gentle, even glow along their entire length, which makes them much easier to record on film than other light sources. They are also usually used in lively color combinations. By carefully selecting your frame or angle, you can isolate and play up certain elements of a neon sign, display, or decoration to achieve an interesting balance in color and shape. By using a telephoto lens or by moving in and shooting at close range, you can even create a colorful abstraction, like the close-up of a red and yellow sign below.

Look for neon lights that are surrounded by darkness; they have richer colors and stand out more dramatically than one in the window of a brightly lighted cafe, for example. Many neon lights can be pictured with a hand-held camera if you use high-speed film, especially when the tubes are brightly concentrated and you are close to them. If a sign has only a few tubes and you are farther away, however, you may have to use a tripod and make a short time exposure. Take your cue from your camera's meter, then bracket by one full *f*-stop in each direction to be sure of getting optimum results. For 160- or 200-speed film, the basic exposure is usually about 1/60 second at *f*/4. With an automatic camera without a manual override, you'll need to bracket by temporarily resetting the film-speed dial at half and at double its proper setting.

A close-up of a soft-drink sign produced an abstract composition with contrasting colors and bright swirling shapes that echo one another.

With this faintly misty shot, Pete Turner not only achieved one of the splendid color compositions for which he is known, but also succinctly conveyed a feeling for the pastime of attending drive-in movies. In case you're wondering, that's Love Story, All About Eve, *and* Goodbye, Columbus *on the bill.*

Besides telling us that a hotel has seen better days, the neon letters in this photograph form a well-balanced arrangement of colors and shapes.

Jeffrey M. Dunn

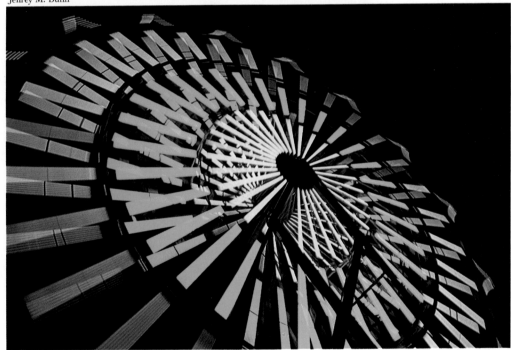

36

An unusual pattern of light bands radiating from a central point was created when a carnival ride, adorned with neon, moved slightly during a short time exposure.

Taillights

With a time exposure at night, a camera can record patterns of moving lights that cannot be seen by the eye. Cars and other motor vehicles are excellent subjects for this photographic sleight of hand. The vehicles themselves often move too fast to be recorded on film during a long exposure, yet their lights leave phantom traces across the scene. Busy roadways become rivers of red and white; a lone car on a roadway can leave a mysterious luminous trail.

No hard-and-fast rules can be given for photographing car lights, since situations vary. But it is best to set up your tripod at locations where the ambient light is not too strong and where vehicles are moving fast – a bridge over a freeway or a tunnel entrance, for example. Since your time exposure will have to be long – from about 5 seconds up to perhaps a minute – plan to use a slow- or medium-speed film and a very small aperture – $f/16$ or $f/22$ – to prevent overexposure. It may even be necessary to use a neutral density filter to reduce further the light reaching the film (see page 202). Because so many variables are involved, plan to experiment with different exposure combinations. For an added dimension to your picture, try jiggling your camera during the exposure.

Colour Library International

Lorna Humes

Light trails left by cars as they enter a tunnel convey a feeling of fast movement that contrasts dramatically with Hong Kong's serene night sky line. The red and yellow dashes in the left roadway were created by brake lights and blinking turn signals.

An intricate pattern of swirling lines reminiscent of a Jackson Pollock painting was created by jiggling the camera while taking an exposure of a freeway.

▶

During a time exposure, a car exiting over a hill left only a trail of glowing red streaks to mark its passage. The cooperation of the driver was necessary, since the car's headlights had to be off to avoid lighting up the lonely roadside.

Michael Newler

Photographing a tunnel interior from a moving car produced this interesting result. The tunnel lights and the lights on other cars were recorded as jiggles and blurs, but the front hood of the photographer's car remained sharp because the camera and the car were moving in unison during the exposure.

37

Sky Lights

Stars and aircraft can also be used to produce intriguing light trails during a time exposure. But successfully capturing either on film requires longer exposures and more careful planning than simply recording the light paths created by landbound vehicles.

Airplane trails are best photographed near an airport, where planes will be flying low and where a series of takeoffs and landings can be recorded in a fairly short time. Using a technique like the one described for taking several bursts of fireworks (see page 120), you can shoot a multiple exposure by simply locking the shutter open and putting the lens cap on between planes. Exposure for a location can be determined only through testing. For a scene like the one shown at right, a good starting point is an aperture of $f/8$ with a 64-speed film.

Recording star trails also requires experimentation, but the basic procedure is simple. Work on a clear, moonless night in an area where there is no ambient light from buildings or street lights. Set up your camera on a tripod and use a cable release to lock the shutter open. The rotation of the earth will take care of the rest because as the earth turns, the slowly shifting position of the stars will be recorded as streaks of light. The length of the streaks will depend on the exposure time, which can last from 15 minutes up to several hours.

For a start, try a one-hour exposure on a medium, 64-speed, film with an aperture of $f/2.8$. Use a wide-angle lens to get a sweeping view. Constellations with bright stars give the best results. The circular paths shown in the picture here were obtained by aiming the camera at Polaris, the North Star, which is situated almost directly over the North Pole. The corresponding reference in the southern hemisphere is the Southern Cross constellation.

Shin Ikushima

The flight paths of several low-flying airplanes heading for a busy commercial airport were recorded as eerie white streaks in the sky.

During an exposure that lasted most of the night, a camera aimed at Polaris, the star above the North Pole, captured the circular traces left by other stars as the earth rotated. In any star trail shot, it is helpful to include a foreground element, such as the branches here, to provide a sense of perspective.

38

Paul Davis

Time Passages

Time-lapse photographs – pictures of the same scene taken over a period of time – are always fascinating because they reveal changes that take place too slowly to be appreciated by the human eye. The time period involved can be a few minutes, a few hours, or a few days. It can even be months. The pictures of the changing seasons at the right, for example, were taken at three-month intervals.

Professionals frequently use elaborate motor drives and interval timers to take time-lapse sequences. But for simple series such as the ones shown here, you do not need any special equipment. You can use a watch as a timer, and the camera need only be mounted on a tripod to ensure that each picture will be framed exactly the same way. It is best to leave a camera in place once you have set it up. If the interval between exposures is so long that you have to move the camera, be sure to mark the height and angle of the camera on the tripod and the position of the tripod on the ground or floor.

If you are making a time-lapse sequence indoors, use the same light source and camera setting for each exposure. An electronic flash is recommended because it gives consistent results. Outdoors, where the theme of your series may be the changing mood of light at different times of the day or year, you will have to vary your settings to accommodate the changes. And to avoid ruining a sequence with one poor exposure, be sure to bracket each picture.

Two exposures –one taken at daybreak, the other at dusk –portray two faces of the New York City skyline as seen from Brooklyn.

James Denis

A series showing the dramatic seasonal changes in a corn field gains added interest because of the boy who appears in the same clothes at the same location in every shot. For such sequences, stakes driven into the ground can serve as markers for placing the subject and the photographer each time.

Stained Glass

Ernst Haas

Too often photographers are captivated by the splendor of stained glass but disappointed by the pictures they take of it. A window that was richly and brilliantly hued as the sun streamed through it becomes washed out and uneven in the resulting photograph. Or a church interior appears more somber and less dramatic than you remember it. With a few simple guidelines, you can take effective photographs that match your recollection of a stained glass scene.

There are actually two different approaches to capturing stained glass on film. A single window or a part of it can be your subject in a portrait, or you can work with the atmosphere of filtered light created by stained glass. When singling out an individual window, avoid shooting stained glass that is being hit by direct sunlight. You can obtain better results on overcast days when the light hitting the glass is soft and even, enriching its colors without creating glaring contrasts. The silhouetting of protective grills behind the windows is also reduced by soft, even light.

A major difficulty in photographing windows is often their high location. Short of using a ladder or finding a vantage point in a choir loft, the best solution is to use a fairly long telephoto lens. A telephoto lens allows you to photograph from a distance, filling the picture area without making the window awkwardly angled. It also lets you pick out details, which are frequently more interesting and dramatic than a whole window. With a 35 mm camera, lenses in the 100 mm to 200 mm range are generally considered to be the most convenient for zeroing in on distant stained glass details.

Capturing the mood that stained glass creates in a house of worship requires a different, much simpler approach. For such scenes, you will usually want to have light streaming through the windows, perhaps catching on dust in the air. The best time of day for such light is middle to late morning or early to middle afternoon when the sun is high but not directly over the building and is hitting the windows at an angle. To capture interior details, be sure to take your exposure reading away from the bright, highlighted areas. A wide-angle lens gives the most panoramic view.

With high-speed film, you often can shoot stained glass and church interiors with shutter speeds that allow you to hand hold the camera. A tripod is advisable, however, if you want to use a long telephoto lens to single out a window or if you want to use a small aperture to obtain greater depth of field. If tripods are prohibited, steady your body against a pillar, or try bracing your camera on the back of a pew. You might also be able to rig a temporary support of hymnals or other objects. If your camera has a self-timer, you can use it to release the shutter gently. It avoids possible camera movement that can occur easily when tripping the shutter with your finger.

Photographer Ernst Haas showed a discerning eye for medieval craftsmanship when he made this close-up photo in England's famed Canterbury Cathedral.

Light pouring through the sloping stained glass windows in the main chapel at the U.S. Air Force Academy in Colorado gives a serene, muted atmosphere to a modern setting.

A close-up of a window figure in a Mexican church reveals the rough-hewn character of the stained glass that is part of its charming primitive style.

40

Photographing Through Glass

Picturing your subjects through glass can result in many interesting effects and original photographs. The glass can be rippled, frosted, or colored in manufacture; fogged by steam or frosted by the weather; or lettered, decorated, or etched with details. As the picture of the window washer at far right shows, even a coating of soapy lather can be effective. Sometimes you will want to use specially manufactured glass prisms or cylinders, which, when held to your camera's lens, distort all or part of your image.

The chief problem in photographing through glass is avoiding reflections on its surface. You can usually do this by changing your camera angle and switching off any offending lights on the camera's side of the glass. In some cases, however, it may be necessary to use a polarizing filter (see page 190). Of course, as you will see on the following pages, reflections themselves can be used to create special effects. And sometimes you may want to juxtapose a reflection with a subject on the other side of the glass.

If glass is rippled, frosted, or hazed over, the subject has to be fairly close to it. If your subject is too far back, it becomes distorted or indistinct. Subjects also work well when they have strong, simple shapes that are readily identifiable, such as those in the picture of the children.

In focusing, you have two choices. You can use a small aperture and keep both the glass and the subject in focus. Or you can use a larger aperture and focus sharply on either the glass or the subject. Each produces very different results.

Bernard J. Bell

Photographing two children through the rippled glass on a shower door produced an image that looks like an impressionistic water color.

The skyline of midtown Manhattan at dusk became sleekly silhouetted against a blood-red sky when it was shot with a red filter. The illusion that the buildings are elongated is the result of a glass cylinder held to the lens during the exposure.

In this picture of a window washer, the strong sweeping strokes of soapy lather on plate glass contribute to an unusually dynamic portrait of a person doing his job.

William N. Seelig

Ray Holden

Props positioned at various distances behind a sheet of frosted glass combined with strong backlighting to produce this unusual still life. The glass surface functions as both a semi-transparent material and a rear projection screen, allowing the camera to record double images of the bottles and glass.

Glass and Metal Reflections

When light hits a smooth, shiny surface, such as polished glass, metal, or plastic, many of the light waves bounce off without becoming scattered, and when we view the surface from the proper angle, we see a reflected image. Such reflections provide you with a marvelous opportunity to give added dimension to a picture by showing two different aspects of the world at the same time. In effect, it's like having a window that opens onto a realm that is usually unseen. And since the reflected image will nearly always be slightly distorted, it may have a surreal, dreamlike quality, as the picture of a cemetery reflected in a woman's sunglasses at left does.

In the most effective shots of reflected images, there is usually some unexpected contrast between the reflection and the actual scene. This can be a contrast in color, shape, or content. Since a reflection offers a second viewpoint in a photograph, it is often helpful to use a reflective surface that is self-contained and provides a natural frame, as in the pictures of the sunglasses at left and truck at right.

The shiny back of a tank truck looks as if it has been painted with a highway panorama as it reflects the roadway and photographer's car behind it.

Angled panels of mirrored glass on an office building break up a reflection of a nearby marquee into a pattern of interesting fragments.

◀

In this poignant photograph, rows of tombstones reflected on sunglasses show what the subject is seeing and suggest what she may be thinking.

42

Abstract Reflections

There is no need to limit yourself to reflections that you happen upon. It is fairly easy to create reflections and manipulate them to achieve effects that are either abstract or highly suggestive. Use any shiny surface that you can shift easily to make it relative to the camera and subject positions. Even soap bubbles are a possibility.

One versatile and easy-to-use surface that is highly reflective is aluminum foil. Smooth or crinkled to various degrees, a piece about 18 inches long taped to a sheet of stiff cardboard can be used to produce a variety of effects. To use it, prop it up vertically against a heavy object on a tabletop, and place a brightly colored subject in front of it. Use a spotlight in a reflective hood to light the subject and increase its color saturation but be careful not to let the light hit the foil. Colored construction paper is a good experimental subject.

The subject and the camera both can be adjusted to obtain the most pleasing effect. The camera should be equipped with a macro lens or a screw-on supplementary close-up lens (see page 182) so that you can work fairly close to the foil. Since you will be shooting at an angle, stop down the lens aperture to $f/16$ or $f/22$ so that you will have plenty of depth of field. Bracket your exposures. Often, a slightly under- or overexposed shot will look better and can be incorporated in a multiple image like the ones described in the section on sandwiching slides (see page 258).

Keith Boas

For this uncommon color reflection, the photographer used aluminum foil that had been slightly crinkled and then smoothed out. Overlapping sheets of blue, gold, and green construction paper, as shown in the diagram at right, were then leaned against a box near the foil.

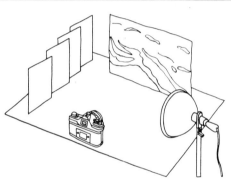

P. Baker/FPG

The shiny surfaces of bubbles show repeated reflections of a young girl. Bubbles are an especially attractive surface because of their multi-hued iridescence. For this effect to work well, the subject should be brightly lighted in a darkened room.

43

When photographing brightly colored reflections in a highly reflective surface such as Mylar, work in a darkened room with just a spotlight for illuminating your props. With no ambient light to cause secondary reflections, you'll have more control producing the effects you want. Since your camera will be focused close and positioned at an angle to the reflective surface, stop down the lens for maximum sharpness.

Mirror Reflections

Of all reflective surfaces, mirrors provide the truest reflections. Indeed, they are so lifelike that, in a photograph, it can be hard to distinguish between the actual scene and the reflected one without some visual clue, such as a frame. The photographer can take advantage of this characteristic to produce some surprising images, including some outright eye-puzzlers, as you can see in the forest scene on page 141. Even when a mirror serves merely to set off and frame another view of a scene, as in the picture of the room at right, it can add an uncanny sense of depth because of the clarity of its image.

When photographing a scene that includes a mirror, you will have to shoot from a slight angle to avoid taking your own reflection. Also, bright light sources reflected in a mirror create glare. It is usually best to use a small aperture and to stand back from the mirror to obtain as much depth of field as possible. This is necessary to keep both the reflected image and the scene surrounding the mirror in focus. You must remember that to keep a subject that is reflected in a mirror sharp, the subject-to-mirror distance must be added to the mirror-to-camera distance when focusing. With most single-lens reflex cameras this is no problem because you can usually preview the depth of field through the lens. With a rangefinder camera, the image in the mirror can be thrown out of focus by setting the camera just for the camera-to-mirror distance.

Another very different effect can be obtained by holding a small hand mirror next to your lens. If the mirror is held at a right angle to the lower half of the lens, it will split the scene and render a slightly distorted mirror image of the scene on the bottom half of the photograph, as in the shot of the sun at far right. That picture was taken with a simple purse-size mirror. To avoid the possibility of getting a double reflection – one from the mirror's glass front surface and one from its mirrored back surface – it is best to use a special mirror silvered on its front surface. One source is the Edmund Scientific Company (101 E. Gloucester Pike, Barrington, New Jersey 08007), which sells a front-surface mirror as part of a trick and special effects photography kit. It is easier to manipulate the mirror if your camera is on a tripod.

Ernest Newsom

To capture this striking combination of eastern and western skylines in a single image, the photographer based exposure not on the predominant part of the scene, but on the reflection of the bright sunset in the car's rearview mirror.

A mirror framing a doorway that in turn frames a wall and a picture creates a great illusion of depth, and the foot in the foreground adds an unexpected human presence.

In this playfully surreal shot, a mirror reflects the surrounding autumnal forest so perfectly that only the white frame of the full-length mirror and the subject's hand thrust out from behind it tell us what is going on.

Doris Barker

The illusion of a setting sun reflected off placid water was created by holding a small mirror against the lower half of the camera's lens. A red filter heightened the mood.

Mirror Portraits

The extra dimension that photographing a reflection in a mirror adds to a picture can be especially useful when taking portraits of people. In its simplest application, if you and your subject stand at an angle to a mirror so that you can see each other's reflection but not your own, you can produce the effect of a portrait already framed and hung.

A more telling picture can be achieved when the scene around the mirror conveys information about the personality of the person, as in the photograph at far right of a woman reflected in the mirror of her memorabilia-laden dresser. And as in the dressing-room photograph, multiple aspects of a person can be shown with a series of mirrors.

Mirrors are also an easy and fun way to take self-portraits. Of course, the camera will have to be included in the scene, but the picture of the man in a rearview mirror demonstrates a technique for shooting without having the camera covering one's face.

A circus funhouse mirror transported to an unexpected sandy location permitted the photographer to take this distorted photograph of a man against a rich blue sky.

Judie M. Ford

Mirrored panels in a dressing room situated both in front of and behind the subject create so many multiple images of her that it looks as if she has been cloned.

Marcia Keegan

A touching portrait of
a former showgirl is
achieved as the mirror
shows her and her
present surroundings
while the pictures in front
of the mirror reveal her
younger days.

By placing the camera at
about eye level, the
photographer was able to
eliminate some guesswork
when he took this self-
portrait in the rearview
mirror of the car. Note
that he set the exposure
for the scene in the
mirror, allowing the
bright scene outside the
windshield to become
overexposed and
washed out.

45

Photographing Through Water

Water is a fluid, transparent medium, and by photographing a subject through it you can produce some unusual results. Shapes are distorted to some degree and may even be completely contorted if the water is turbulent, as in the picture at right below of a car going through a carwash.

If your subject is submerged, your main challenge, as when shooting through glass, is to reduce surface reflections. At midday, when the sun is directly overhead, you will usually have little trouble finding a camera angle that is free of most reflections. If you place a polarizing screen on your camera's lens (see page 190), you'll also reduce annoying water reflections in most situations.

Water reflections are not always deterrents, however, to achieving fine photographs. Small amounts of reflections, especially from slight surface disturbances or bubbles in the water, can even be helpful in creating a delicate mood of overall lightness, as they are in the photo at left.

Some interesting effects can also be achieved when your subject is only partially submerged. A person floating in a still pool with only head and shoulders above water often seems to have an elongated body. Someone with long hair lying down in the calm, shallow waters of a wading pool or bathtub, face above water, will be surrounded by a soft spreading halo of floating hair.

If you want to take a camera into water to get a picture like the ones of the swimmers here, you need a special protective underwater housing or else a camera specially designed for photographing underwater.

J. Simmerman/FPG

By positioning a camera in a waterproof housing half in and half out of the water, the photographer was able to get this dynamic shot of a swimmer in action.

© 1981 Bill Binzen

Water cascading over the windshield of a car going through a carwash produced this unusual rippled distortion.

◀
Bubbles in the water enhance the playful exuberance of a happy young swimmer. They also act with surface ripples to create reflections that contribute to the picture's cheerful mood.

David Bowles

46

Water Reflections

As painters and photographers have long known, water is the preeminent source of reflections, offering far more possibilities than other reflective surfaces. On a calm day, any sizable body of water can become an enormous mirror, reflecting almost perfect images of clouds, rainbows, boats, buildings, mountains, and foliage along embankments. At times, in fact, the reflected image can be so accurate that you can produce a stunning eye-puzzler, such as the photograph of a ladder at far right.

Since water is liquid, it can also fragment reflections. Barely perceptible surface undulations can result in an image with impressionistic overtones, whereas slightly more pronounced ripples can turn a scene into an almost abstract collage of colors. And like larger bodies of water, puddles and wet pavement provide endless possibilities for creative picture taking.

Water is most reflective when the sun is low in the sky in the early morning or late afternoon. And the best time to find glass-smooth water is just after dawn, before the sun has a chance to warm up the air, causing breezes.

Sonja Bullaty/The Image Bank

© 1981 Bill Carter

A rain-drenched manhole cover becomes a gleaming, vibrant red field as it reflects a multitude of city lights. When you are photographing wet pavement at night, neon signs, movie marquees, and traffic lights all make good color sources.

Keith Boas

After shooting a distorted reflection of a sailboat in water, the photographer turned the picture upside down to heighten the impressionistic mood.

Michael deCamp/The Image Bank

Because reflections in rippled water are blurred, it is best to work with scenes that have bold, contrasting colors and interesting compositions. Here a pond reflects autumn foliage.

In this surrealistic photograph, the clouds are mirrored so perfectly in glass-smooth shallow water that the ladder on its surface seems to be suspended in the sky.

Lens Flare

Lens flare is one type of reflection that photographers usually try to avoid. It is light reflecting off the outer and many inner surfaces of the camera lens. This reflection produces a glaring spread of light, aptly called flare, that has probably ruined millions of pictures. But when used carefully and monitored through the viewfinder of a single-lens reflex camera, flare can produce spectacular results.

Lens flare can convey the blinding presence of the sun. It can also give a scene a soft, almost foggy diffuseness that can tone down a cluttered background or create a light high-key mood.

Although manufacturers today go to great lengths to prevent flare with multiple anti-reflection lens coatings, it is still fairly easy to produce. Simply having the sun – or another intense light source – in a scene is likely to cause flare. It often happens when the sun is just outside a scene and its rays are picked up and reflected by the front of the lens. A lens hood is ordinarily used in such situations to prevent flare, so it is important to leave it off. A wide aperture, $f/2$ or $f/2.8$, also increases the effects of flare, as does any device that spreads the light entering the lens, such as a soft-focus lens attachment (see page 186) or a diffraction grating (see page 208). Indeed, just putting a filter on a lens, especially a filter that is smudged or dirty, increases the chances of flare.

Determining exposure is tricky with flare. Your camera's meter translates the presence of bright light into an exposure that will reproduce the scene as darker than normal. With very bright flare, it is easy to underexpose a scene by three stops or more, producing a low-contrast, nearly silhouetted subject. And unless you are trying to create a moody low-key shot, it is best to determine the normal exposure for the scene by pointing your camera away from the source of the flare. Then manually set the exposure according to that reading and disregard the meter when the flare reappears in your viewfinder. On automatic cameras you may have to use your exposure override switch or temporarily change the camera's film-speed dial to compensate (see page 36).

Ken Biggs

The sun setting behind a rugged outcrop of rocks created this beautiful circular form of lens flare. The effect was enhanced by the use of a magenta-colored filter over the lens (see page 194).

Carolyn L. Cline

Often the most lens flare occurs when the sun is just outside the scene and creates a soft, misty diffuseness, as in this golden-toned, high-key rendering.

The blinding intensity of the sun is immediately conveyed by the lens flare in this photo of a soaring sea gull.

Special Situations **149**

Selective Focusing

A photograph that is needle sharp from edge to edge is not always the most desirable. Unless the subject is simple and the arrangement harmonious, a picture with every detail sharply in focus is likely to appear cluttered.

One very effective way to single out a subject from its surroundings is to limit the depth of field – the zone that your lens keeps in sharp focus – so that the subject is sharp and the other elements are out of focus and fuzzy. You can choose to blur the foreground or the background, a detail or the main subject. Sometimes you may even want to blur both. But in any case, the viewer's eye will nearly always be drawn immediately to the subject when it stands out as the sharpest element in the picture.

Depth of field is affected by three factors: the aperture you select, the subject's distance from the camera, and the focal length of your lens. The wider the aperture you choose, the more limited the depth of field you will get, so it is best to use a large aperture, such as $f/2.8$ or $f/2$, for selective focusing. Similarly, the closer you focus on a subject, the more limited your depth of field becomes. If you focus on a subject only 3 or 4 feet away, the depth of field may extend only a few inches, whereas with a subject 10 or 11 feet away, it may extend for several feet. The third factor, the focal length of the lens, affects depth of field: the longer the focal length, the more limited the depth of field at a given distance. Although you can limit depth of field with any lens, this means simply that you will get the most limited depth of field with long telephoto lenses, even at less than a wide-open aperture.

The key to taking a good selectively focused photograph is to make your out-of-focus elements as blurred as possible. For maximum blurriness, there should be a substantial distance between your subject and the background or foreground elements you want to blur. With such distance, you can be sure these elements won't fall within

Michael Kay

No matter how small, a subject that is sharp stands out against an out-of-focus background. Without question, the bird is the center of attention.

the lens's zone of sharpness. It is especially important to blur foregrounds as much as possible because it can look like a mistake if they are only slightly out of focus. You may have to move to within a few inches of your foreground to transform it into a soft, suggestive frame, as shown in the picture of the balloons at lower right.

With the wide apertures necessary to obtain selective focus, you will often have to use fast shutter speeds. And this can be a problem if you discover on a bright day that you do not have a shutter speed that is fast enough to avoid overexposure. One way to reduce the light entering your lens is to use a neutral density filter (see page 202).

Sonja Bullaty

In portraits, selective
focus is especially useful
to subdue distracting
backgrounds and focus
attention on the subject.
In this photograph, the
vegetation was far enough
behind the girl to merge
into a blurred backdrop
of harmonious green tones.

© 1981 Bill Carter

Blurred balloons not only
create a soft, colorful
frame for this view of
Disneyland, but they
also convey an amusement
park atmosphere.
Foreground elements
work best when they are
considerably out of focus.
Use a wide aperture, focus
on your distant subject,
and move close to your
foreground frame.

49

Special Techniques **151**

Blurring: Unfocused Subjects

Sometimes the essence of a scene is best conveyed by a subject that is blurred rather than one that is sharp. Striking and unusual results can often be obtained simply by adjusting the focusing ring on your camera to throw a subject deliberately out of focus. One of the most immediately noticeable occurrences is that highlights begin to soften and spread. If the highlights are brightly colored, they will become suggestive smears of color – an effect that can be heightened by turning the focusing ring *during* the exposure. An interesting side effect of the tendency of out-of-focus light to spread occurs when a subject is strongly backlighted.

To control the effect of an unfocused subject, it's best to use a single-lens reflex camera so that you can look through the lens and monitor the degree of sharpness in the viewfinder. Although you can throw a subject out of focus at nearly any f-stop, it is much easier if you use a wide aperture, such as $f/2$ or $f/2.8$, which limits the depth of field. It is also easier if you use a normal or telephoto lens, both of which have more limited depths of field than wide-angle lenses. Pick strong, simple subjects and try to isolate them against a plain, distant background. Make sure the subject is out of focus enough so that your effect is obviously intentional, but not so much so that the subject is completely unrecognizable.

Michael Newler

By setting your camera's lens deliberately out of focus, you can achieve a mystical quality in which highlights spread and details blend into soft smears of color. For the maximum out-of-focus effect, limit the lens's depth of field by usng a wide-open aperture.

▶

A woman and child against sparkling water became softly blurred silhouettes surrounded by mysterious white rings when recorded with an out-of-focus mirror telephoto lens. A characteristic of a mirror lens is that it turns out-of-focus highlights into rings rather than spreading pools of light (see page 42).

Dennis Hallinan/ALPHA

50

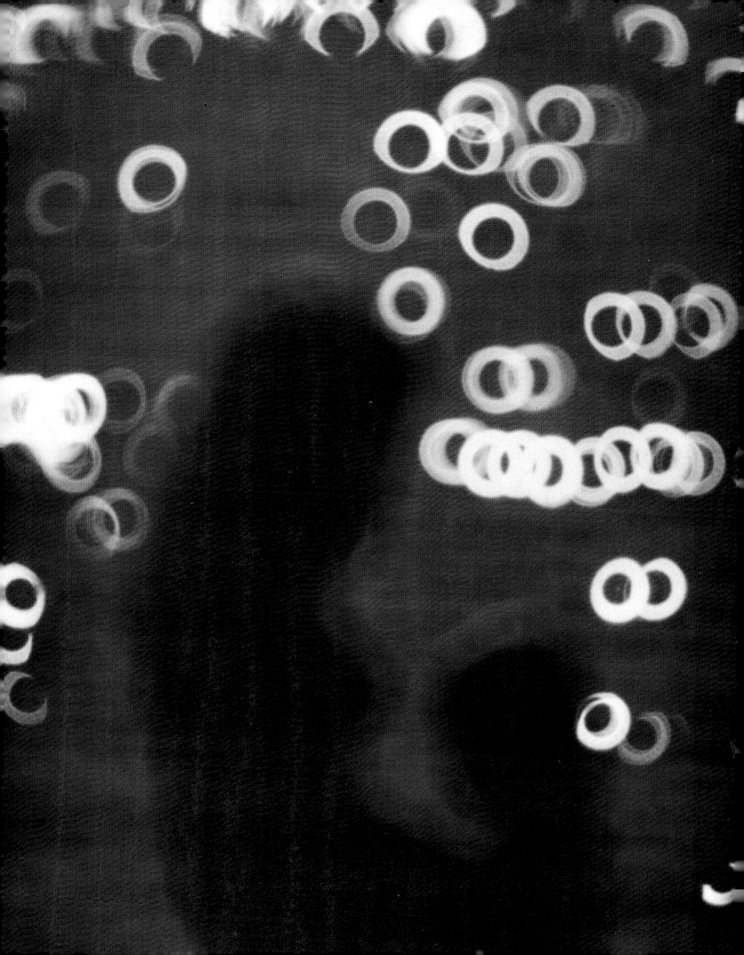

Blurring: Moving Subjects

One of the most effective means of suggesting movement in a photograph is to allow a moving subject to become blurred. It not only approximates the way our eyes perceive a fast-moving object, such as an airplane propeller, but it also turns the subject into a soft, suggestive presence.

To record a moving subject as a blur, you must use a slow shutter speed, but the exact slowness depends on several factors. The speed of the subject is most crucial. A speeding automobile may become blurred during a 1/500-second exposure, whereas an ambling pedestrian may require 1/30 second. The angle at which you photograph your subject and your subject's distance from you is also important. A subject passing across your field of view blurs more quickly than one headed straight toward you. Also, a close subject blurs more than a distant one moving at the same speed. And for much the same reason, a telephoto lens that appears to bring a subject closer produces blurring more easily.

All of these factors must be gauged against the amount of blur you want to achieve. The slower the shutter speed you use, the more blurred your subject. In general, first estimate the shutter speed needed to freeze your subject. Then use a shutter speed about half as fast to get a blurred but still recognizable image of the subject. For example, you can usually freeze a walking subject at 1/125 second and get a reasonable blur at 1/60 second. Of course, your aperture will have to vary with the shutter speed you select. And if your speed is 1/30 second or longer, use a tripod.

With slow shutter speeds on a bright sunny day, you run the risk of overexposure. Use a slow-speed film and have a neutral density filter (see page 202) handy. If you have a camera with automatic exposure control, switch it to manual or shutter-priority mode. If your camera can only be used in an aperture-priority mode, setting it for a small aperture will often give you a slow enough shutter speed to create blurring, especially if you are using slow-speed film. On a fully automatic camera, cover your lens *and* meter with a neutral density filter.

Norman Kerr

Frank Townsend

Figures blurred during a 1/15-second exposure convey the circular movement of people at play while focusing attention on the young boy at the center. Note how the boy at right is less blurred than the other figures because he is moving toward the camera, rather than across its field of view.

In the faint light of dawn, gently rocking Venetian gondolas were recorded as blurred yet identifiable images during a three-minute exposure. Their images create a muted frame for the buildings in the distance.

Against a placid pastoral backdrop, a car was reduced to ghostly streaks, suggesting that it was moving much faster than the posted speed limit.

Photographer Ernst Haas
used strong backlighting
from a setting sun and
reflections off water, as
well as a slow shutter
speed, to create this
evocative photograph.

Ernst Haas

Jiggling

You can create visually dynamic pictures with stationary subjects by moving your camera during a long exposure. One of the best subjects for such unorthodox treatment is lights on signs, buildings, and roadways at night, as they trace delicate paths on the film. In daylight, a scene with multiple highlights, such as sparkling water, can produce similar results. Subjects with bright colors, such as the flowers here, can turn into almost abstract smudges of soft, muted hues.

    Sometimes the amount of movement that occurs naturally when you hand hold a camera during a long exposure is enough to produce an intriguing amount of blur. At other times, especially when trying to create light traces, you may want to jiggle the camera or wave it up, down, and around, as the photographer did in the abstract image of lights at lower right. But remember that even slight camera movements will be greatly exaggerated on film. A faint quiver of the camera in your hands during a 1/15- or 1/8-second exposure may produce a subject that is just barely recognizable.

    With a tripod, it is possible to use camera movement in a more carefully controlled manner, particularly during longer time exposures at night. One common technique is illustrated by the picture of a skyline here. For about half of a time exposure, the camera is left still to record a strong basic image. During the remainder of the exposure, the camera is slowly and smoothly moved in one direction. In this case, it was moved upward to create long blurs on the bottom of the image that emphasize the vertical lines of the buildings. An interesting effect can also be achieved by moving the camera in a stop-and-start fashion, creating a series of hard images with faint traces between them.

    Whether controlled or not, the results of camera movement are often unpredictable. And because of the long shutter speeds involved, exposure is somewhat a matter of guesswork. It is essential to experiment by taking several pictures of a scene with various exposure settings. Even at night, you probably will find it easier to work with slow-speed film. During the day, you may also need a neutral density filter (see page 202).

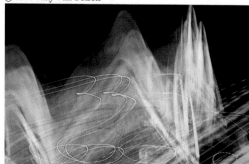

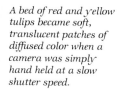

A bed of red and yellow tulips became soft, translucent patches of diffused color when a camera was simply hand held at a slow shutter speed.

Waving the camera slightly during a hand-held exposure with a slow shutter speed turned the sign for a popular fast-food outlet into an abstract pattern of lights.

David William Hamilton

David Hamilton created this gleaming, elongated image of Chicago's skyline by a carefully controlled movement of a camera on a tripod during an exposure of several seconds. For the first half of the exposure, the camera was left still. During the second half, it was slowly swung upward to produce the light traces at the bottom of the picture.

A one-second hand-held exposure produced this unusual evening view of London's Big Ben. The humanlike form on the right was an unplanned addition to the picture. It is a rapidly approaching bobby, about to arrest the photographer for lying on the sidewalk.

Jay Edward

Freezing Action

Just as a slow shutter speed is the chief means of blurring motion, a fast shutter speed, at the other extreme, is the primary tool for stopping action and producing a sharply detailed image of a moving subject. The 1/1000- and 1/500-second settings on most modern adjustable 35 mm cameras are capable of freezing nearly all normal activities, including many that happen too quickly to be perceived by the eye. A person appears suspended in midair. Water drops seem frozen in space. Extremely fast shutter speeds can also let you capture the essence of a fast-moving event or preserve an elusive moment of beauty.

A good stop-action picture requires planning. If you know or can foresee the path that your subject will follow, you should determine your camera angle, lighting, background, focusing distance, and exposure in advance so that you can concentrate on your subject. You can track a moving subject easily because fast shutter speeds relieve worries about camera movement. But it is necessary to anticipate the moment of peak action you want to freeze. Make a conscious effort to press the shutter a split-second before that instant occurs to allow for the microseconds required for your finger to respond to your brain's command.

When working with very fast shutter speeds, it is almost always best to use high-speed film, ISO/ASA 400, which allows you to set your camera for smaller-than-maximum apertures, thus gaining more depth of field. If the light is so dim that it prevents you from using the shutter speed you prefer, consider having your film push-processed for a one-stop-higher rating (see page 49). Also, if you are shooting in dim light, remember that you probably can freeze your subject with slower shutter speeds if you back away from it. If you make your picture from a head-on or oblique angle rather than letting the subject pass directly across the camera's field of view, you also have a better chance to freeze the action. In addition, slower shutter speeds can be used to capture subjects during momentary pauses – a swing at the top of its arc or a dancer at the height of a leap.

Michael Page

With an exposure of 1/500 second, the photographer was able to stop the motion of a bird in flight at just the instant its wings were pointed downward, forming a striking triangular composition.

54

▶
The excitement of a kayak shooting rapids during a race was captured with a fast shutter speed that froze the churning water.

B. Laire

Electronic Flash

Jim Cassemus/ALPHA

Electronic flash can stop action better and produce even more surprising images than a fast shutter speed in ambient light. When you use electronic flash as the main light source, the duration of the burst of light from the flash replaces the shutter speed as the chief determinant of exposure time. The duration of a flash, which is measured in thousandths of a second, ranges from as fast as the camera's top shutter speed to many times faster.

Electronic flash units vary widely in the intensity of their light output, in the time it takes them to reach full capacity after each picture, in the special features they offer, and in their exact modes of operation. But they basically fall into two categories: manual and automatic. Manual flash units–or automatic units in the manual mode–emit an unvarying burst of light lasting about 1/1000 second. You determine exposure with a table or calculator dial usually found on the back of the flash unit or with guide numbers supplied by the flash manufacturer. Guide numbers are determined by the power of the flash and the sensitivity of the film. You divide the flash-to-subject distance (in feet) into the guide number to find the f-stop you need for a good exposure. For example, you might be using a film with a speed of ISO/ASA 100 and a flash unit that has a guide number of 80 for film of that speed. If your subject were 10 feet away, you would need an aperture of $f/8$ ($80 \div 10$). If the flash-to-subject distance were 5 feet, you would use $f/16$ ($80 \div 5$).

The increasingly popular automatic flash units actually vary the duration of their light output to suit the subject's distance. They have a built-in light sensor that, when the flash goes off, measures the amount of light bouncing back from the subject to the flash. The sensor shuts off the flow of light when the film has received enough exposure. With a close subject, the flash duration can be as short as 1/50,000 second. Most units can be set to operate with two or three different f-stops.

With an automatic flash unit and a close subject, you can take advantage of the extremely brief duration of the flash to get stop-motion shots that were once possible

only in the laboratory. With subjects that are closer than 2 or 3 feet, however, you will need a macro lens or a supplementary close-up lens (see page 182) and a flash unit that accepts a special remote sensor, commonly called a macro sensor.

Freezing action with flash can sometimes be a problem with single-lens reflex cameras and some rangefinder models. These cameras have a focal-plane shutter, a curtain that passes just in front of the film. Cameras with these shutters synchronize electronic flash only at shutter speeds of 1/125, 1/90, or 1/60 second and slower, depending on the camera. (Check your camera manual for specific instructions.) If you use a slow shutter speed to take a flash

As with ordinary stop-action photographs, freeze-motion pictures taken with a flash must be planned. For this photo, the photographer had to find the best location and camera angle and also anticipate the instant when the skateboarder would be upside down.

With an automatic flash and close-up equipment, it is easy to freeze fast action, even a drop of water, as the duration of the flash with a subject at close range is very brief.

picture of a moving subject when there is a lot of ambient light, you will get a blurred image (ghosting) of the subject in addition to a sharp image frozen by the flash. If you want sharp and clear action shots, the only solution is to shoot when the ambient light is not strong – outdoors at dusk or indoors in a dimly lighted room. Ghosting is not a problem with the leaf shutters used on many medium format and most 35 mm rangefinder cameras because you can use a shutter speed fast enough to prevent ambient light from recording on the film. The flash will synchronize with these shutters at any shutter speed.

55

Fill-In Flash

Although including ambient light in a flash photograph can be a problem when you are trying to freeze action sharply, there are many other times when it can be advantageous. The most common situation occurs when you use flash as a fill-in light to soften harshly shadowed areas in a daylight picture. As the two twilight pictures on the opposite page show, a flash fired during a time exposure of a dimly lighted scene can also illuminate a foreground subject. City skylines, bridges strung with lights, and lighted monuments and buildings at night all make good backgrounds for time exposures with fill-in flash. And as the picture of the children with sparklers shows, the possibilities of flash with long exposures are numerous.

When illuminating a foreground with flash, make sure that your subject is well separated from the background so that the flash does not create shadows. Your subject should remain still to avoid creating a secondary ghost image from ambient light hitting it – although slight ghosting along the edges can sometimes be very effective.

For long exposures, your camera must be on a solid support such as a tripod. To determine exposure settings, first find the *f*-stop for flash in the usual manner (see page 164). Then take a meter reading to determine the exposure time for that *f*-stop. If you are shooting outdoors with no reflective surfaces nearby, use an aperture of at least one half-stop wider to compensate for light lost through dispersal.

J. W. Myers/FPG

Electronic flash units

During a time exposure that captured the exuberant pattern of moving sparklers, a brief burst of light from a flash froze the images of the two youngsters who were wielding them.

56

Robert Clemens

This handsome portrait was taken with flash during a time exposure. When the flash was fired at the beginning of the exposure, a sharp image of the model was recorded on the film. Then, while the shutter remained open to register the dim background, she moved slightly, creating faint ghosting.

Mary Lorenz

While the camera's shutter stayed open for several seconds to record the beautiful afterglow of a sunset, a flash lighted up a gnarled shoreside tree, creating an almost surreal juxtaposition.

Painting with Flash

With dark scenes too large to be illuminated by one burst of light from a flash, a single flash unit can do the work of several when used in combination with a long exposure time. The technique is known as painting with flash. All it requires is that you walk around to illuminate different parts of the scene, one at a time, while the camera's shutter is open.

Painting with flash is an ideal method for lighting large interiors, such as auditoriums and churches, as well as many exterior scenes. Outdoors at night, it can also be used to make a snow or beach scene look as if it were bathed in moonlight. And if you want to create a puzzling multiple-exposure self-portrait like the photograph on the opposite page, simply fire a flash at yourself in one part of the scene and then repeat the operation in another part.

For the time exposure, you need a tripod and a cable release that will let you leave the shutter locked open on the B setting for several minutes. Shoot only scenes that are *very dark,* and if there is any ambient light at all, use slow-speed film to avoid overexposure. The flash unit does not have to be wired to the camera because you will be operating it manually by pressing the test or open bulb button, which lets you fire the flash independently of the camera.

Plan to light the scene as evenly as possible. Avoid overlapping flashed areas and stay the same distance from all the areas you are illuminating, except where you might want to move in slightly to highlight a center of interest. Use the average flash-to-subject distance to determine the correct *f*-stop as you normally would with a flash in manual mode: divide that distance into your flash guide number (see page 164). If the scene is so large that you have to set off the flash inside the scene itself, hide behind furniture, cars, or shrubs so that you won't appear as a ghostly silhouette in the final picture – unless, of course, that's the effect you're after. Always be aware of the camera's position and aim your flash away from the lens to avoid flare.

Keith Boas

By comparing these two pictures, you can readily see the advantages of lighting a large nighttime scene with several bursts from a flash unit. In the photo at left, the only illumination was from a single burst of flash positioned near the camera. In the picture above, the photographer set the camera on a tripod and locked the shutter open. Then, during an exposure that lasted for about 5 minutes, he walked around the scene and fired the flash into seven separate areas –from four spots along the foreground periphery and three in and around the greenhouse.

57

Mark Engbrecht

In this creative application of the painting-with-flash technique, the photographer included himself in the scene three times by setting off a hand-held flash in his face at each spot between gas pumps. In addition, he lighted the whole scene with a flash when he was not in it.

Filtered Flash

Michael deCamp/The Image Bank

The quality of the light produced by an electronic flash is about the same as sunlight at midday, and with proper exposures it will yield lifelike colors with daylight-balanced film. For special effects, however, the color of light from a flash can be altered by placing a filter over the front of the flash. You may want to use a filter with a slight color cast to create a mood in a picture – to give a golden hue that simulates warmth, for example, or to give an icy blue tinge to a wintry scene. You can also use filters with more pronounced colors to produce even more exciting results.

The advantage of placing a filter over a flash rather than over the lens (see page 194) is that you can be more selective about the parts of a picture to be colored. Only the areas illuminated by the flash will undergo a color shift; as the picture at far right shows, any ambient light will not be affected. When using multiple flash, or when using the painting-with-flash technique described on page 168, you can use different colors in different parts of the scene, as in the multihued still life at right. There are limitations in the use of a filtered flash, however. It can be used with only a relatively dark scene and with subjects that are fairly close at hand. You cannot change the color of the sky or a distant mountain, as you can with a lens filter.

Some manufacturers offer accessory color filters for their flash units, but you can also buy sheets of tinted gelatin that are used for theater lights and tape them over your flash unit. These filters are usually available at theatrical and art-supply stores. Or you can use acetate color printing (CP) or gelatin color compensating (CC) and light-balancing filters available through photo dealers. For subtler hues, you can make your own filters by coloring matte acetate sheets with water colors, crayons, or photo retouching colors (see page 266).

When using a filtered flash, you must adjust your exposure to compensate for the light absorbed by the filter. As a rough guide, when a filtered flash is the primary light source, increase your exposure two f-stops for a red filter, one and a half f-stops for green or blue, and one f-stop for light blue, orange, or magenta. Make no change for a yellow filter.

To create this unusual multicolored still life, the photographer set up an arrangement of white objects on a beach at night and lighted the scene with a series of electronic flash units covered with filters of various colors.

The pressure and intensity of an air-traffic controller's job were very effectively conveyed by lighting him with a flash equipped with a red filter. Note that none of the other light sources in the room was affected by the filtered light – as they would have been with a lens filter.

58

Wide-Angle Lenses

The view of a normal lens, the lens most cameras come with, approximates the way our eyes see the world in image size and in the relative positions of objects. However, these factors change when the focal length of a lens is much shorter or longer than normal and when a lens is positioned at a vantage point closer to or farther from roughly the same scene. When these things happen, our brain, which is used to judging spatial relationships the way our eyes see them, is presented with an optical illusion.

As the pictures here and on the following two pages show, a wide-angle lens, a lens with a short focal length, takes an expansive view of the world, increasing the apparent distances between objects. And as illustrated on pages 176 to 179, a telephoto, or long, lens does just the opposite, creating a compressed view of reality.

On a 35 mm camera, whose standard lens is 50 mm, the focal lengths of wide-angle lenses vary from a near-normal 35 mm down to an encompassing 6 mm, which presents a circular fisheye view of the world. The apparent distortions created by wide-angle lenses are greater with lenses of shorter focal lengths. But even the popular moderately wide lenses (35 mm to 24 mm) offer many opportunities for creatively manipulating a scene.

All wide-angle lenses exaggerate the distances between objects close to and farther away from the lens. Objects close to the lens seem magnified to larger-than-life size, whereas more distant forms appear rapidly smaller. Usually this characteristic is used to give a scene a greater sense of depth or to make a subject appear longer or taller.

By picking a low, oblique camera angle, you can greatly heighten an effect called keystoning with a wide-angle lens, which makes the bottom of a subject look inordinately large and the top almost minuscule. With an ultra-wide lens, the result can become grossly exaggerated, as seen in the photo of the Eiffel Tower on page 175.

Wide-angle lenses are usually avoided for close-ups of the face because the tendency of the lens to enlarge near and diminish more distant subjects results in a bulbous distortion. Yet a wide-angle lens can be used effectively to create a caricature.

With wide-angle lenses, you should

not encounter any special problems in determining exposure or in focusing. In fact, such lenses provide excellent depth of field, and most have a fairly wide maximum aperture. You can also achieve an ultra-wide-angle effect with a special fisheye supplementary lens. It increases your viewing three or four times over that of the prime lens, depending on which manufacturer's accessory you use. With a normal or wide-angle prime lens, it's possible to obtain a 180-degree angle.

The enormous size of a cutout of Lenin in Moscow was emphasized by shooting from a low angle with a wide-angle lens. This combination made the figure's head very small in comparison to its base, turning it into a looming presence.

Norman Kerr

Keith Boas

Wide-angle lenses

A chessboard vividly demonstrates the distortions that are created by a 16 mm, full-frame fisheye lens. Note how the squares in the front are curved, whereas those farther back are rectilinear. Note also the great difference in size between the toppled pawn in the front and the one at the rear edge of the board.

59

A grin is heightened to absurdity by a wide-angle lens's distortion. To create this caricature, the photographer used an 18 mm lens on a 35 mm camera positioned approximately 2 inches from the subject's face.

Neil Montanus

Viewed upward from almost ground level with a 16 mm wide-angle lens on a 35 mm SLR camera, a young soccer player's outsized legs and soccer ball convey the essence of the kicking sport.

David William Hamilton

Even a much
photographed tourist
attraction can be given a
novel appearance with an
ultra-wide-angle lens.
Here photographer David
Hamilton used the
extreme keystoning that
such a lens can create to
make the Eiffel Tower
look unexpectedly short
and squat.

With its 180-degree view,
a fisheye lens captures
the intensity of the
moment as two rugby
teams prepare to go head
to head in a scrum.

Gerry Cranham

Telephoto Lenses

Steve Dexheimer

Whereas a wide-angle lens gives the illusion of expanding space, a telephoto lens seems to compress it, making objects appear much closer together than they actually are. This is easy to understand if you keep in mind the simple rule of perspective: the farther objects are from the eye, the shorter the apparent distance is between them.

This rule is immediately evident, for example, with a row of receding fence posts; there is a lot of space between the first few posts, but the amount of space diminishes rapidly until in the distance there is little or none at all. Because a telephoto lens magnifies objects, enlarging a part of the scene taken in by our eyes, it causes those objects to appear closer than expected.

The ability of a telephoto lens to compress distance makes it one of the most creative tools in the photographer's bag. It can be used to make a line of airplanes appear to be almost on top of each other, to exaggerate the curving lines of a bridge, to dramatically enlarge the sun behind a cactus, or to convey the packed intensity of a motorcycle rally.

In focal length, telephoto lenses for 35 mm SLRs range from about 75 mm to over 1000 mm. Each doubling of the focal length doubles the magnification and consequently halves the apparent spatial relationships in the resulting image. Thus, the effect of spatial compression is greatest with the longest lenses.

Lenses over 200 mm, however, tend to be expensive, usually require a tripod, and are not very practical for everyday photography. One less costly way to obtain a longer focal length is to use a device known as a tele-extender – an optical accessory that fits between an SLR camera body and a prime lens. Tele-extenders come in various magnifications. A 2X extender, for example, doubles the focal length of a lens, whereas a 3X triples it. Thus, a 135 mm lens, a handy, moderately long lens for a 35 mm camera, will become a 270 mm lens when it is used with a 2X extender. High-quality extenders are designed to couple fully with a camera's built-in exposure system.

Tele-extenders do have some shortcomings. Most notably, they reduce the amount of light reaching the film. A 2X extender, for example, cuts the light by two f-stops; if you are using a prime lens with a maximum aperture of $f/4$, the effective maximum aperture with a 2X extender becomes $f/8$. In addition, images may not be as sharp as with a telephoto lens of equivalent focal length, especially along the edges of the image. To improve sharpness, you should stop the lens down two or three stops from its widest aperture, thereby increasing depth of field, which is restricted, as it is with a regular telephoto lens. To compensate for a small aperture, use a high-speed film and possibly a tripod for the slower shutter speeds that may be required.

Telephoto lenses

A telephoto lens allows a photographer to zero in on action and convey the feeling of crowded intensity by making the subjects look closer together. Here a 200 mm telephoto lens on a 35 mm camera compressed the distance effectively in a battle for the lead.

60

Sunrise and sunset are always good times to use a telephoto lens because it makes the sun look surprisingly larger and lets you silhouette a subject, such as the cactus here, against a great golden disc.

Thomas S. Momiyama

Lined up on a runway, the U.S. Navy's famed aerobatic Blue Angels appear to be a single multiwheeled vehicle. The illusion was created by a telephoto lens.

The apparent compression of space by a telephoto lens causes curves to look much steeper. In this case, it makes a bridge with a gentle rise look more like a roller coaster.

Geri Biondich

Zoom Lenses

Unlike regular lenses, which have a fixed focal length, a zoom lens has special movable optical elements that can shift in relation to each other to vary the focal length, thus making your subject appear larger or smaller. Along with the regular aperture and focusing controls, a zoom lens has a control for adjusting focal length. If you move that control during an exposure, you can get some extraordinary results because the size of your subject changes while it is being recorded on film.

The most common result of this technique, called zooming or racking, is the appearance of strong lines radiating out from the center of interest, which can give a striking sense of motion. Zooming can also produce stunning patterns when applied to time exposures of lights at night.

To make a zoomed photograph, you must use a slow shutter speed – no faster than 1/30 second and preferably longer. Usually you need to use a tripod to avoid any additional camera movement during the long exposure. But you can hand hold the camera during an exposure of 1/15 or 1/30 second if you have a zoom lens on which the focal length is controlled by sliding the lens barrel straight in or out rather than by rotating it. If you hold the camera against your face to brace it, you'll find it easier to slide the lens barrel. Because the center of the image will show less of the effect and therefore appear sharpest, it's usually best to center your main subject.

For a strong streaked-motion effect, you need a background with a mixture of bright and dull colors or highlights and shadows. Zoom through the full range of focal lengths for maximum results. How fast or slow you zoom also has a great effect on the outcome. You also can pause at the beginning or end of a zoom to freeze a sharper image of the subject. Depending on the lighting conditions, you may need to use slow-speed film and a small aperture to prevent overexposure from the slow shutter speeds necessary.

Grace Lanctot

Zoom lens

By zooming the lens during a long exposure, the photographer transformed a static scene into one with radiating lines that suggest hurried movement. An 80 to 200 mm zoom lens was used with a very short hesitation at the 80 mm setting before zooming to the 200 mm end of the focal scale.

Although football is a dynamic, fast-moving sport, it is often difficult to capture the explosive action in a still photograph. Here zooming the lens during a 1/30-second exposure gives a sense of excitement to what could have been an ordinary photograph.

© 1973 Judith Gefter

Zooming with bright, small light sources at night can produce interesting light trails, especially when the lights are varied and colorful. This picture was photographed from an airplane over Miami, Florida.

61

Macro Lenses

Extreme close-ups are among the most fascinating photographs, whether they provide an intimate view of plants and insects or simply enlarge some common house object to a still life with sculptural elements. Since most camera lenses will focus only as close as two or three feet, however, you need special close-up equipment to get really close to your subject. Nearly all of that equipment is designed to be used with a single-lens reflex camera. When you are working at close range, framing is difficult and the depth of field is limited, often to a fraction of an inch; you need the through-the-lens viewing system of an SLR camera to handle these problems effectively. Also, when you magnify a subject, any camera movement during exposure is magnified proportionally. For camera steadiness and sharper results, use a tripod.

There are a number of ways to obtain a close-up. The simplest, and least expensive, is to use supplementary close-up lenses – auxiliary lenses that look like filters and screw into the filter threads of your prime lens. They are available in different strengths of magnification – usually marked as +1, +2, or +3 – and can be combined for greater magnification.

Another way of taking close-ups is to use extension tubes or bellows. Both are hollow devices that fit between the camera body and lens to extend the lens positioning and thereby increase its magnifying power. Extension tubes come in various fixed lengths to provide different magnifications, and the best models couple the lens with your camera's exposure system. Bellows are more flexible, allowing you to adjust the magnification over a wide range. But they are bulkier and much more costly and usually require that you operate your camera manually.

With any device that merely adapts a regular lens for close-up work, there is likely to be some loss of image quality. You can partly compensate for this by using a smaller aperture. But if you are seriously interested in close-up photography, you will probably want to get a special close-focusing, or macro, lens, which is designed especially for working at close range.

The most popular macro lenses for 35 mm SLRs have a focal length around 50 mm, like a normal lens, but their focusing

rings permit lens extension until a subject is enlarged to about half life size on film. Greater magnifications are obtained by using the macro lens with extension tubes, bellows, auxiliary close-up lenses, or tele-extenders (see page 176). Macro lenses can be used to take pictures at normal distances as well – although their relatively small maximum aperture, typically $f/3.5$, limits them to fairly bright situations. Macro lenses also have special "flat-field" optics so that they can be used to copy flat, two-dimensional subjects such as stamps, pictures, and slides without distorting them, as regular lenses sometimes will.

In a close-up of flowers, strong backlighting can reveal the delicate translucence of the petals.

Macro lens and bellows

Carole Honigsfeld

Michael Newler

This comparison shows how a lens attachment that produces very heavy diffusion can literally add atmosphere to a picture. The picture at left, which was taken without the soft-focus attachment, is a straight documentation of a marina. With the attachment, the scene is instantly shrouded in fog, as shown above.

Soft-focus attachment

The soft, romantic mood created by a diffusion lens attachment is heightened by the contrast between the light and dark areas of this photograph.

64

Vignetting Attachments

Another special effect that can be desirable for certain pictures and can be achieved with a lens attachment is vignetting. In a vignetted photograph, only the center of the image is sharp. Around the edges, the image gradually fades into a solid tone or an area that is softly diffused. Vignetting is primarily a framing device. When you tone down or eliminate the surrounding scene, your subject literally becomes the center of interest. Whether it be a building, a landscape, or a person, the subject immediately captures the viewer's eye because of its sharpness.

The most subtle effect is obtained when the edges are diffused, forming a soft-focus border that is not immediately apparent. The effect is achieved in much the same way as the overall soft-focus effect described on page 186. There are many commercially available screw-on vignetting attachments, including adjustable ones with leaf shutters providing a variable opening, that produce a sharp center – or even off-center – image surrounded by diffused edges. You can also produce the effect by smearing a thin coating of petroleum jelly around the edges of a UV (ultraviolet) or skylight filter or by placing a coin on a filter when you coat it with artist's matte finish spray.

With a square filter holder on the front of your camera's lens, you can also vignette by using a sheet of matte acetate with a small hole cut in the center. This technique works best with telephoto lenses, which have a shallow depth of field that will blur the hard edge of the cutout area. Normal and wide-angle lenses tend to show the edge. With any lens, however, you can soften the edge somewhat by keeping the acetate as close to the lens as possible and by using a wide aperture. As with overall diffusers, there is no need to make an exposure adjustment because most of the light reaches the film.

A light-tone vignetting frame is produced by cutting a center hole in a material that is translucent but not transparent. This material can be a piece of thin matte acetate slipped in a square filter frame or a piece of facial or lens-cleaning tissue temporarily taped over the lens. In a similar manner, gelatin filter squares can provide a vignetted border in any color.

To obtain a black frame or border in a vignetted picture, you have to use a totally opaque material such as construction paper. The side facing the lens should actually be black to prevent light reflecting into the lens and causing lens flare and loss of contrast. Determine your exposure before placing your vignetting device over the lens. Otherwise, your meter is likely to be influenced by the dark area and produce an overexposure of the central image. If you have an automatic camera, see page 36 for an explanation of exposure adjustments.

Petroleum jelly on a UV filter

Michael Newler

*In this picture, the
dramatically vaulting
architecture of the opera
house in Sydney,
Australia, was isolated
by a vignetting
attachment that diffused
the edges of the scene.*

*Used carefully, a
vignetting lens attachment
that softly blurs the edges
of a scene while leaving
the subject sharp can
simulate the way we see
when we concentrate
on detail.*

Polarizing Screens

Of all the lens attachments that a photographer can own, the one that offers the greatest versatility in achieving creative effects is a polarizing screen. This filterlike attachment can be used not only to remove or lessen unwanted reflections from nonmetallic surfaces but also to deepen the color of the sky, minimize haze, and enrich the colors in a scene. In short, it can often elevate an ordinary snapshot into a spectacular photo.

Light waves normally vibrate in many directions at once. But when they are reflected from a nonmetallic surface such as water or glass, most of the light waves become polarized – that is, they vibrate in just one plane. A polarizing screen works by blocking this polarized light. The screen consists of tiny crystals that act as though they were aligned in parallel rows like the slats of a Venetian blind and block light not traveling in a plane parallel to the rows. The filter rotates in its holder, and when turned so that the rows are at right angles to the polarized light being reflected by a subject, the reflected light is completely blocked. In other positions, the filter can transmit a portion or all of the reflected light.

Light is reflected not only by shiny surfaces, but also by tiny particles in the air. This light is the source of haze and much of the sky's brightness. Since a good part of this light is polarized, it can be eliminated with a polarizing screen, thus causing haze to disappear from the image and making the sky darker and bluer. In enriching colors, polarizing screens work by eliminating glare, highlights, and other surface reflections.

Polarizing screens are easy to use. With a single-lens reflex camera, you can see the exact effects in the camera's through-the-lens viewing system. With a rangefinder camera, hold the screen up to your eye and turn it until you get the effect you want. Then mount it on the lens with the mark or handle on the screen's rotating ring in the same position. The maximum effect is usually achieved when the mark or handle is pointing toward the main light source.

For darkening the sky and reducing haze, the filter is most effective when the sun is at a right angle to your camera, sidelighting your subject. And for eliminating reflections, the most effective camera angle is one that equals the angle between the light source and the reflecting surface – about 38

Patty Van Dolson

degrees above and to the side of the surface.

A polarizing screen blocks more than half of the light entering your camera, requiring you to use an exposure one and one-third stops greater than you would have to without it. But on most modern cameras, the light meter's sensor is located behind the filter, and the camera's meter automatically indicates the light loss. However, if your subject is sidelighted, you will be at a right angle to the sun, and you should manually increase the exposure one half-stop so that the shaded half of your subject is not underexposed. And if you are using the polarizer just to tone down a reflection rather than eliminate it completely, you should add an additional half-stop to make up for the brightness the reflection can cause.

Shot through a polarizing screen, a weather-bleached remnant of a tree is dramatically set off against a darkened sky.

When this antique-shop window still life was photographed without a polarizing screen, as at far left, light reflecting off the glass gave the scene an overall haziness and reduction in contrast. A polarizing screen, used for the photograph at left, eliminated most of the reflection and increased color saturation.

Polarizing screen

These two pictures show the polarizing screen's amazing ability to deepen the color of the sky. The photo at left was taken without a polarizing screen. The version above was taken with the screen, making the roof's overhang more prominent in appearance.

66

Color Polarizers

Many lens attachments are designed to add color to an image. By far the most common, as we will see on the following pages, are color filters. But an unusual adaptation of the polarizing screen, known as a color polarizer, not only adds color to a scene, but also lets you vary this color in a continuous and gradual manner.

The simplest color polarizer lets you change the intensity of a single color. A red one, for example, will let you go continuously from a faint pink to a deep red, as this series of the Washington Monument demonstrates. Amazingly, the other type of color polarizer allows you to change from one color to another. A red-yellow version, for example, goes from deep red to lighter red, through various shades of orange, and finally to bright yellow.

Both types of color polarizers have two components – a rotating front element that is a grey polarizing screen and a stationary rear element that is a more specialized polarizing screen with crystals that alter the color of light when the front screen is rotated. It is somewhat similar to the color changes that polarized light produces on larger crystals. For practical purposes, the difference between the two types of color polarizers is that single-color ones let you make very subtle variations in the intensity of a color, whereas the shifts with two-color polarizers can be more sudden and intense. Also, when two-color polarizers are used, you can obtain some very unusual results with reflections because of the ability of polarizing screens to block light from reflections. With a red-to-blue polarizer, for example, you can capture pink highlights on blue water; with a red-green one, you can get pink windows in a predominantly green scene.

There is a price to pay for all this versatility, and that is a great reduction in the amount of light reaching the film, especially when a color polarizer is turned to its maximum setting. There can be a loss of nearly three f-stops with a filter on a deep red setting. In most cases, of course, your camera's meter will indicate the changing exposure values. But to avoid needing a tripod, you should use a color polarizer on a bright day or with medium- or high-speed film.

Derek Doeffinger

Rotating the front element of a red-to-green color polarizer can produce a deep red sunset, a yellowish one, or, as here, an unexpectedly green one.

Color polarizer with two components

John Fish

This series shows the effects of using a single-color red polarizer. The picture at top left of the group was taken without the polarizer. The picture below it was shot with the polarizer set on the faint pink end of the scale; the picture at top right shows the effect at the midway point. The one at bottom right was made at maximum red.

Color Filters

The easiest way to alter the hues in a scene – and transform the mood it conveys – is to place a color filter over your camera's lens. The most common and durable filters available are the glass disks that screw into the filter threads on the end of your lens. These filters come in different sizes to match the diameter of your lens; with adapter rings, they can be used on lenses of different diameters. There are also some fairly inexpensive filter systems consisting of a square filter holder that attaches to the lens and a wide variety of drop-in plastic filters and other lens attachments. Gelatin sheets, too, fit into a frame and slide into a square filter holder.

Most filters fall into four categories. The most widely used were designed to alter the contrast of colors reproduced as grey tones in black-and-white photographs. Their color and color intensity are designated by a number. A No. 11 filter, for example, is yellow-green; a No. 29, deep red. Color compensating, or CC, filters are another type of color filter. They are made in the three primary colors – red, blue, and green – and in the three complementary colors – cyan, yellow, and magenta – and they are available in graduated densities. The density and color of a CC filter are designated by a number-letter abbreviation. CC10M, for example, indicates a magenta filter with a slight (10 percent) density; CC50R represents a strong (50 percent) density of red.

Because they are available in low densities, CC filters are especially suited for making subtle changes in a scene. Another advantage of CC filters is that you can combine them to increase the intensity of a single color. If you don't have a CC30R filter, for example, you can get the same effect by using a CC20R and a CC10R together. And you can combine two filters of different colors to obtain a third color. Avoid using more than two filters, however, because with more than two, the amount of light scattered by their surfaces results in a noticeable loss of sharpness.

Special yellow- and blue-tinted filters known as light-balancing filters are the third common type. These filters are designed to modify the color of light from a scene so that a film will give natural-looking results when used with light for which it is not correctly balanced. A yellow-orange No. 85B filter, for example, lets you shoot tungsten-balanced film in daylight or with an electronic flash, whereas a blue No. 80A lets you shoot daylight film with tungsten light. But you can obtain some interesting effects if you deliberately misuse these filters. If you use a blue light-balancing filter with daylight film outdoors, for example, you will get a pronounced blue effect, which is often just right for a water or snow scene.

Finally, to fill the gaps left by the three types of standard color filters, there are special filters designed to produce vivid offbeat hues such as aqua, rose, and purple.

All color filters work by transmitting light of their own color and blocking the light of other colors in varying degrees. The amount of light blocked varies with the color – yellow, even deep yellow, blocks relatively little light. Deep red, green, and blue block a lot. This blockage requires that you must increase your exposure to compensate for the loss, either with a larger aperture or a slower shutter speed. Today the adjustment is often provided by the filter manufacturer in f-stops. But it is traditionally expressed as a filter factor – a number that indicates how much the volume of exposing light must be increased. For instance, a filter factor of 2 tells you that you must double the amount of light – that is, increase the exposure one f-stop.

As long as your camera's light sensor is positioned so that it is behind the filter, the camera's meter will sense the loss of light and try to compensate for it. But camera meters are designed to respond to white light, and they can be misled by light that is saturated with one color. In addition, films differ in their sensitivity to colors, and filters affect light from different light sources differently. The best advice is to bracket by shooting at least a full f-stop more and less than the one indicated.

Keith Boas

68

A deep magenta filter on a wide-angle lens gave a surreal ultramodern feeling to this photograph.

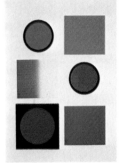

Color filters

As these comparison photos show, a dark blue color filter can transform a scene from day to night.

Ken Biggs

Neil Montanus

In this scene, a medium
green filter silhouetted a
sea gull and gave the
water attractive yellow
highlights.

A flattering light amber
filter not only enhanced
the warmth of the setting
sun in this picture, but it
also gave a golden tone to
the sand and enriched the
hues of the woman's
blonde hair and red
dress.

Neil Montanus

A deep blue filter
transforms almost any
daytime scene into one
that looks as if it was
taken in the late evening.
But the most realistic
results are obtained when
you shoot with a light
blue or medium blue filter
around twilight, the
time this photograph
was taken.

Paul Kuzniar

An almost colorless scene photographed on a heavily overcast day was transformed by an amber filter into a memorable souvenir of Greece. In fact, the presence of the clouds made the resulting color all the more intense.

Patty Van Dolson

A magenta filter gave this sunset a rich vibrant color. The filter absorbed so much light that the entire surrounding scene appears to be shrouded in darkness.

An orange filter on a
very wide-angle lens gave
a tide-washed shore a
glowing sheen and
rendered the highlights
a brilliant shade.

Ken Biggs

198

Split-Field Filters

When you start adding color to photographs, you'll find that some scenes benefit from adding more than one color or having color in only part of the image, an advantage split-field filters can provide. Many of these filters offer two-color combinations – for example, half-blue–half-red. On other split-field filters only one-half is colored, often with a graduated boundary so that the colored half softly merges into the clear area.

Half-color–half-clear filters are primarily useful for changing the color of the sky. It is usually just a matter of positioning the filter so that the demarcation between the areas coincides with the horizon, and you instantly have a golden sky or brilliantly red sunset without affecting the rest of the scene. Two-color filters can also be used this way, and a yellow-purple or an orange-blue filter is particularly handy. As the street scene on the opposite page shows, the purple or blue half increases the saturation of the sky, while the orange half warms the foreground. A red-blue filter can also be useful for producing a sunset-reddened sky over deep blue water, for example, or for adding color to a drab scene, as the comparison at far right below shows.

Like solid-colored filters, split-field filters are available as either conventional screw-in filter disks or as square plastic filters that slip into a filter holder. When buying them, remember that you can get a two-color effect by simply combining two half-color filters. Doing this is more expensive, but it gives you more flexibility in choosing color combinations; and the area where the two colors come together is usually more gradual. There are also half-filter versions of color polarizers (see page 192) that let you vary the color effect in just half of the picture.

With gelatin squares, of course, you can make your own split-field filters. In fact, just by holding a piece of gelatin filter over the lens, you can change the color in part of the scene. Gelatin filters can also be taped over a clear haze or UV filter if the tape does not appear in the image area. They can also be placed in a gelatin filter frame and used in a square filter holder. If you are using two or more filters, however, be sure to butt them together evenly along their edges to avoid an unfortunate clear gap or dark overlap.

Ken Biggs

On commercial two-color filters, both halves have about the same filter factor so that the scene will be evenly exposed. If you make your own filters, strive to select filters of fairly even density for even exposure. With a filter that colors only half the scene, you will usually place the filter over the sky or some other bright element, so base your exposure on the unfiltered part of the scene by taking a reading of the scene before putting the filter over the lens, and using that reading to set your exposure. The demarcation between the two areas of color or between the filtered and nonfiltered areas should be as blurred as possible, usually requiring a shallow depth of field, best achieved with a fairly wide aperture on a telephoto lens.

A deeply saturated No. 25 red gelatin filter butted together in a filter holder with an equally strong No. 47 blue gelatin filter produced the bold colors in this tropical scene.

Paul Kuzniar

Katherine Winn

A street scene in Marrakesh, Morocco, was dramatically transformed by two half-color split-field filters with graduated edges.

Split-field filter

The famous statue Christ of the Andes overlooking Rio de Janeiro was so shrouded in mist that the picture above is almost monochromatic. Photographed through a red-blue split-field filter at left, the sky took on a rosy glow and the mountain's shadows became deep blue.

69

Neutral Density Filters

Neutral density, or ND, filters are simply neutral grey filters that reduce the amount of light entering the lens. Unlike color filters, ND filters do not change the color balance of a scene. Their effect is similar to selecting a smaller aperture or a larger shutter speed.

Because of their ability to control light, ND filters can expand the creative potential of a camera. Selective focusing and blurred action (see pages 150 and 154), for example, can be achieved in bright light with an ND filter. A neutral density filter can also be used with a wide aperture, permitting you to limit your depth of field to isolate a subject sharply between an out-of-focus background and foreground, even in bright light. In addition, as the comparison photographs of the barn illustrate, a special split-field version of the neutral density filter affects only half of a scene and can be used to darken the sky or another bright part of a view without changing its color.

As the table here shows, neutral density filters are available in a wide selection of densities, and they can be combined to obtain in-between densities. The more popular ones range from a 0.10 density to a 1.00 density. In this range, the easiest ones to use are the 0.30, 0.60, and 0.90 densities, which reduce exposure by one, two, and three stops, respectively. But for special effects, particularly with long time exposures, you may need a filter with a much greater density.

Keith Boas

Approximately the same number of cars were passing when these two highway photos were taken, but in the one above, a neutral density filter allowed the photographer to use an exposure time so long that the moving vehicles were not recorded on film. Exposure for the first picture was 1/250 second at f/8. In the second picture a 3.0 neutral density filter permitted an exposure time of 12 seconds at the same aperture. The exposure time included the equivalent of a one-and-a-half-stop increase to allow for the reciprocity effect.

Neutral Density Filters

DENSITY	FILTER FACTOR	LIGHT TRANSMITTED	EXPOSURE INCREASE (F-STOPS)
0.10	1.25	80%	$\frac{1}{3}$
0.20	1.6	63%	$\frac{2}{3}$
0.30	2	50%	1
0.40	2.5	40%	$1\frac{1}{3}$
0.50	3.1	32%	$1\frac{2}{3}$
0.60	4	25%	2
0.70	5	20%	$2\frac{1}{3}$
0.80	6.25	16%	$2\frac{2}{3}$
0.90	7	13%	3
1.00	10	10%	$3\frac{1}{3}$
2.00	100	1%	$6\frac{2}{3}$
3.00	1,000	0.10%	10
4.00	10,000	0.01%	$13\frac{1}{3}$

Neutral density filter

70

Col. Noel A. Grady, Jr.

Keith Boas

Your camera's meter ordinarily senses the loss of light caused by an ND filter and indicates when the camera is set for correct exposure. But with a time exposure of 1 second or more, the light sensitivity of nearly all films begins to decline, and in the case of color film, there is also a shift in the color balance. So if you use an ND filter to obtain a long exposure, compensate by increasing your camera's indicated exposure – preferably by increasing the *f*-stop because increasing exposure time complicates the problem further. With color film, corrective filters can adjust for the color shift, and with black-and-white film, an adjustment in film development time is also suggested. Such phenomena are commonly known as reciprocity effects (see page 48). If you are using an ND filter so dense that you can't get a reading on your camera's meter, take a reading without the filter and multiply it by the filter factor for your filter. Then adjust for the reciprocity effect.

A neutral density filter allows you to use a slow shutter speed in bright light, capturing the streaked blur of a racing downhill skier.

This comparison demonstrates the usefulness of a split-field neutral density filter, used on the bottom picture only, which can darken the sky or another portion of a scene without changing its overall color. Like many half-filters, it has a soft gradation between areas. Determine your exposure before putting on the filter to ensure a natural rendering of the unfiltered part of the scene.

Special Equipment **203**

The Harris Shutter

With a simple homemade device, you can use color filters to produce spectacular multicolored results. The Harris shutter, as the device is known, uses gravity to pass three color filters in rapid succession in front of your lens. Anything that moves during the exposure is recorded in variegated colors, whereas the rest of the scene appears natural.

In effect, the Harris shutter makes three exposures of a scene, each through a different colored filter. The reason stationary objects look natural is that the three filters transmit, sequentially, the primary colors in white light – red, green, and blue. Each filter lets in the parts of the light blocked by the other filters, so the cumulative effect is about the same as if the scene had been exposed without filters. Anything that moves during the exposure, however, will be recorded in multiple colors because its position is different with each filter. The Harris shutter can lend tricolor beauty to a wide variety of moving subjects – from crowded street scenes to swaying trees or crashing surf.

As the diagram shows, the Harris shutter consists of a long filter strip that fits inside a narrow box. The box is attached to your camera's lens, and the filter strip is pulled up and dropped in front of the lens while the camera is set for a time exposure.

To make an exposure, set the camera on its B shutter setting. Then, holding the solid lower part of the filter strip against the front of the lens, open your camera's shutter. When the action you want to record is happening, simply drop the filter strip. Then close your camera's shutter. The time it takes for the filters to pass in front of the lens is roughly equivalent to 1/30 second. Take a light reading to determine the aperture for a shutter speed of 1/30 second. Use this *f*-stop as your normal exposure. Next try additional shots at one and two *f*-stops both larger and smaller to cover any variation you might have in your equipment or method of use.

It's best to use a color negative film when using the Harris shutter for better exposure latitude. And if the color balance in the negative is slightly off in the part of the scene that didn't move, it can probably be corrected during printing. If you want slides, you can either copy the resulting color prints on color slide film or have slides made from your processed negatives.

Robert Harris

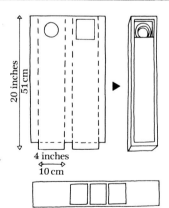

To make the Harris shutter, you need three 75 mm (3-inch) square gelatin filters – No. 25 red, No. 61 deep green, and No. 38A blue. The other materials needed are black cardboard, black masking tape, and an adapter ring to fit your lens. The exact dimensions are not important, just make sure that the box is light-tight except for the opening at the top and on the front. Also, make sure that the filter strip fits fairly snugly but can still fall freely between the adapter ring and the front of the box.

20 inches
51 cm

4 inches
10 cm

Harris shutter

71

Norman Kerr

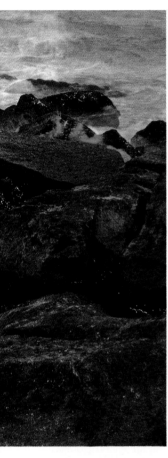

Exposed through a Harris shutter, the stationary rocks were recorded in their natural hues, but the churning water was transformed into bright primary colors by the device's filters.

The three filters on the Harris shutter pass in front of the lens fairly fast. With slowly moving subjects, you will get just rainbowlike edges, as on the front dancer here. But if your subject is moving very quickly, as the rear dancer was, you can record almost completely separate images –each in a different color.

Star Attachments

When we look at a scene with small, intense points of light, whether it be a glistening body of water or candles on a birthday cake, they seem to glimmer and appear more prominent than they actually are. One special group of lens attachments – usually called cross-screen or star filters – breaks up these light points into long starlike flares to convey the effect we see.

Commercially available cross-screen attachments have, as the name implies, a grid of fine lines etched on their surfaces. When one of the intersections on the grid coincides with a point of light, the light flares out along the lines, creating a four-rayed star effect. The space between the lines varies; in general, the finer screens are best for reproducing the effect of a group of small sparkling highlights, whereas the more widely spaced screens will produce cross flares from only the brighter points of light.

Most cross-screen attachments are designed to rotate in their mounts so that you can turn them to get the best effect. In addition, there are variable cross screens with two screens that rotate against one another to produce an eight-rayed star pattern. (You can get similar results by putting one cross-screen attachment in front of another one.) In addition, there are cross screens with triangular grids that create six-pointed stars, and ones with parallel lines that produce a straight flare cutting through the light source.

You can also obtain a cross-screen effect by putting a piece of ordinary window screen in front of your lens. The image will not be as crisp, but if you want a slight soft-focus result along with a star pattern, it can be extremely effective. You can hold the screen in front of the lens or cut a piece to fit into a filter-frame holder or adapter ring.

When using a cross-screen attachment, you need an intense point of light. Night lights are usually best because the flare stands out against the darkness. Also, the closer you are to the light, the greater the effect will be, as long as the light source remains a small point. Two other important factors are aperture and lens focal length. A large lens opening, or a telephoto lens, tends to soften and spread the flare, whereas a small aperture, or wide-angle

Dale Newbauer

lens, tends to sharpen and narrow it. A medium aperture, such as $f/5.6$ or $f/8$, is usually best.

On a single-lens reflex camera, you can monitor the changing effects through the viewfinder by pressing the depth-of-field preview button. To use a cross-screen attachment on other cameras, hold the screen to your eye, turn it to get the effect you want, and put it on the lens in the same position.

No special exposure adjustment is needed with most commercial cross-screen attachments. If you use window screen, anticipate a half-stop loss or so of light for each layer you use. If your camera has behind-the-lens metering it will automatically compensate for the loss.

In this spectacular night shot, the modern lines of the Pacific Design Center in Los Angeles are enhanced by the flare radiating from the street lights. The scene was photographed through a cross-screen attachment that produces eight-point star patterns.

Greg Gronaas

Keith Boas

Bright highlights on a waterskier's wake sparkle like scores of jewels when photographed through a cross-screen attachment with a fine grid.

Cross-screen attachment

A large four-pointed flare, produced by putting a piece of window screen in front of the lens, heightened the holiday atmosphere of this single light. The overall redness comes from the light, not a filter.

72

Rainbow Attachments

Another lens attachment that can produce stunning effects with intense points of light is a diffraction grating. It is more popularly known as a rainbow attachment because it breaks the light up into a prismatic array of colors. A diffraction grating is a plastic sheet with thousands of precisely spaced ridges on its surface; when a strong point of light hits these ridges, they act exactly like a prism, separating, or diffracting, the light into a color spectrum.

The effect and the amount of color produced depend on the spacing and arrangement of the ridges, as well as on your camera angle and the intensity of the light source. Diffraction gratings can create rings or burstlike patterns around a light source or a single streak going through it. Others – much like a cross-screen attachment – produce spokes emanating from the source. Still others create a multicolored pattern.

A variety of diffraction gratings ready to mount on your camera are available from photo dealers, and – like cross-screen attachments – they rotate in their mounts to vary the effects. You can also buy the plastic ridged sheets themselves and use them in a square filter holder just as you use gelatin filters. Some sources are Edmund Scientific Company (101 East Gloucester Pike, Barrington, New Jersey 08007) and Spiratone, Inc. (135–06 Northern Boulevard, Flushing, New York 11359).

Diffraction gratings work best when you have an extremely bright and fairly small point of light in a relatively dim scene. Night scenes are by far the most dramatic. Diffraction gratings do not require an exposure adjustment, but changing the size of the lens opening varies the effect. With most single-lens reflex cameras, you can see the changing effects by pressing the depth-of-field preview button. With other cameras, you can't control the effect as precisely, but you can see the general result with your eye before mounting the grating on the lens in the orientation you've chosen.

Grace Lanctot

Grace Lanctot

Photographed through a diffraction grating that produces a prismatic display on either side of the light source, the brilliantly rimlighted edge of a cloud gained two companion rainbows.

The nighttime skies above the Space Needle tower in Seattle, Washington, came alive with color when the scene was photographed through a Spiralite Rayburst Streaker.™ This diffraction grating produces subtle secondary images with spectral colors.

Diffraction-grating attachment

Neil Montanus

The sleek appearance of a glass-walled office building in Brasilia was emphasized when a radial diffraction-grating attachment turned the sun's reflection into flaring spokes of color.

Stan Oslowski/FPG

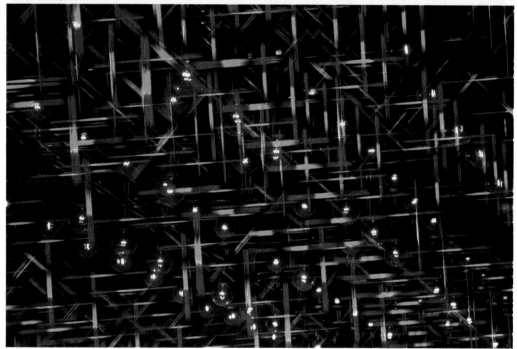

A diffraction grating, like a cross-screen attachment, produces its greatest effect when aimed directly at point sources of light.

Multiple-Image Attachments

Of all the devices you can put on a camera lens, the ones that most startlingly transform a scene are multiple-image attachments. These thick supplementary attachments are sometimes known as prism lenses, and much like prisms, they have angled surfaces that create repeated images of a subject.

As the pictures here and on pages 212 and 213 show, a multiple-image attachment can turn a single building into a city skyline or show a person with many clones. It can also make someone appear unexpectedly elongated. One special version of the multiple-image attachment can even make a still object look as if it were moving.

The arrangements in which multiple-image attachments present repeated images vary greatly. One common pattern is a central image encircled by repeating images. Other arrangements present three images side by side or slice up the picture like a pie to present two, three, four, or even a kaleidoscope of six images.

One of the most striking effects can be achieved with an attachment that causes secondary images of the subject to look like vibrations. One half reproduces the subject normally, while the other half is divided into several narrow bands that create the visual echoes. The attachment can be used to suggest motion or to create a curious elongation. A similar attachment is designed to impart a feeling of very rapid motion. Slightly more than half of the attachment is flat glass, delivering a sharp image of the subject, and the rest has been specially ground to refract light and stretch the image. This creates blurred streaks like those produced when a moving object is photographed at a slow shutter speed.

When using multiple-image attachments, look for isolated subjects against a plain background to avoid cluttered results. Night scenes can be especially rewarding because the darkness disguises distinctions between the images. Be sure to use a single-lens reflex camera so that you can see the effect in the viewfinder.

The lens and aperture you select when using multiple-image attachments are also important. A telephoto lens spreads the images, cutting off part of them around the picture edges. This may or may not be desirable, depending on the effect you prefer. A wide-angle lens pulls the images together

Grace Lanctot

and may show the edges of the multiple-image attachment as a vignette. In addition, its greater depth of field, especially at small apertures, tends to make the demarcation between the images quite pronounced. In general, the best choice is a normal or moderate telephoto lens set on a large aperture. The large aperture will make the repeated images somewhat fainter and less sharp than the main image, but it's simple to stop down the aperture while using the camera's depth-of-field preview button until you achieve the balance you want.

Exposure is no problem with multiple-image attachments because they are clear and transmit nearly all of the light in a scene. Some multiple-image attachments, particularly the circular repeating variety, lend themselves to the use of color filters. You can use small pieces of gelatin filters to color the secondary images and leave the main one natural, as in the picture of the hotel sign at lower right. Or you can color the entire group of images by covering each surface with a different gelatin filter, as the photographer did to make the picture of the Temple of Heaven above. When filtering only a portion of a multiple-image attachment, take an exposure reading without the filter to determine your camera setting so that the main image will be properly exposed. If you want to use different color filters over different images, treat them as you would a split-field filter (see page 200) – that is, make sure they all have the same filter factor, and take your reading through the filters.

Showing multiple hues as well as multiple images, this unusual view of the Temple of Heaven was created by putting a gelatin filter of a different color over each face of a multiple-image lens. Each filter was held in place by tabs of tape along the attachment's rim. A wide aperture was used to soften the lines where repeating images merge.

Multiple-image attachments

Trudee Hess

Dale Newbauer

To give this Balinese performer the aspect of an Eastern deity, two of the multiple-image attachments that produce visual "echoes" in part of the scene were used together. One was almost vertical to create the repetitions of her side, and the other was obliquely angled, causing repeated heads.

This stunning photograph was made in much the same manner as the picture of the temple at left above, but with two important differences. The filter pieces that fitted over the faces of the multiple-image lens were all the same color, and the center face of the five-faced lens was left clear.

Keith Boas

Norman Kerr

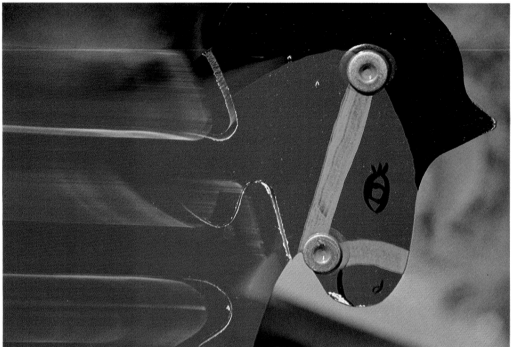

A special attachment that refracts light to produce dynamic streaks in half of the image made a child's common dream seem to come true, transforming this hobby horse into a speedy steed.

Robert Foor

To emphasize the drama of firefighters in action, a multiple-image attachment was used that delivers a repeating image in narrow linear bands.

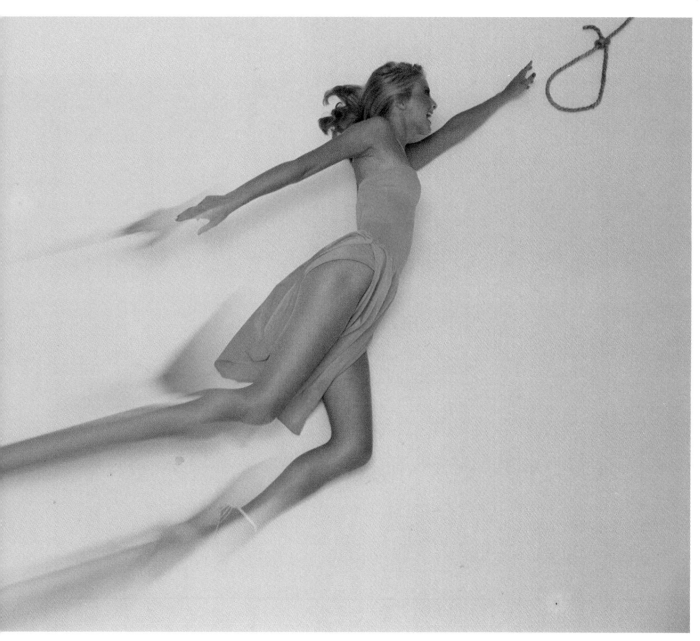

The impression that this model is being stretched out as she rushes to grab a rope was produced by a special prism attachment that elongates half of the image. The illusion is a double one: the model was actually lying on her side on a piece of background paper and the camera was overhead.

Black-and-White Grain

Film is carefully crafted to give the best possible image quality in a wide variety of situations. But just as the extreme sharpness of a top-quality lens can be softened by a diffuser, the characteristics of film can be deliberately manipulated to achieve creative results. This is especially true when you exaggerate the characteristic known as grain—the mottled, pebbly texture that usually becomes visible to the eye only when a photograph is greatly enlarged. In black-and-white pictures, grain gives an image an intense graphic quality, somewhat like a drawing done in charcoal on rough-textured board. As such, it produces interesting results with subjects as diverse as portraits, landscapes, and scenes that lend themselves to journalistic photographs.

Grain in black-and-white photographs is the result of the way film is made and processed. The film emulsion contains a coating of light-sensitive silver compounds. When the film is processed, areas in this coating that have received light during exposure are chemically transformed into tiny particles of metallic silver, creating a visible image. Individually, these particles are too small to be seen by the unaided eye, but they tend to join together in irregular clumps that show up as the distinct specks we call grain. Although manufacturers have made great strides in reducing graininess, the greater sensitivity of high-speed films is largely the result of having bigger light-sensitive particles. Thus, if you want to produce a grainy image, start with high-speed film, such as Kodak recording film 2475, which has a rating of ISO/ASA 1000.

Processing can have a definite effect on the graininess in film. Push-processing (see page 49) increases image contrast and therefore the apparent speed of the film. A by-product of push-processing is increased grain size. By far the easiest way to get a grainy final image, however, is to have an oversized enlargement made of all or part of the photograph and then copy a portion of it with a macro lens or other close-up equipment (see page 182). The amount of magnification you need, both in the enlargement and in the copy, varies greatly depending on how grainy the initial negative is and on how much graininess you want to achieve. The only way to determine this is by experimenting.

Paul O. Guffee

The granular texture produced by grain makes the horses in this classic composition look almost as if they were statues.

Like many pictures with exaggerated grain, this photo was made by blowing up a small section of a negative.

Keith Boas

Even a prosaic scene like the one rendered in this photograph of a train can be transformed by grain, which suppresses details and gives the image a timeless quality.

◄ *Pronounced graininess gives a dreamy quality to the portrait on the opposite page.*

Susan King

Color Grain

The effect of purposely exaggerating the graininess of film in color photographs is quite different from that in black-and-white pictures. Rather than taking on the graphic quality of a pencil or charcoal rendering, a color enlargement of grain more closely resembles the work of certain Impressionist painters. Using a technique called pointillism, Impressionist painters such as Edouard Manet and Georges Seurat carefully applied dabs of paint to canvas to obtain forms that from a distance are easily recognizable but up close are reduced to component dots of colors. A coarse color grain in photographs, as in pointillist paintings, is effective for portraits as well as for broad vistas.

Grain in color pictures is formed in much the same way as in black-and-white photographs, but the specks we see are clumps of dyes instead of metallic silver. As with black-and-white graininess, the grain will be more pronounced if you use high-speed film. And you will get even more grain if you use a high-speed slide film such as Kodak Ektachrome 400 film and push-process it to an exposure index of 800 (see page 49).

The technique for ending with a grainy blow-up of a portion of a color photograph is the same as for black-and-white pictures. You need to get an oversized enlargement of all or part of an image, and then copy a small section with a macro lens or other close-up equipment (see page 182). If you are working with a slide and want the final image to be a slide, you can also use a bellows attachment or extension tubes to make an extreme enlargement of a portion of the image by following the slide copying techniques described on page 250.

For extreme magnifications of tiny areas within a slide, you might consider using a microscope. In addition to the microscope itself, you'll need a single-lens reflex camera body and an adapter to link it to the microscope's optical system. For copying the image, use a color slide film balanced for your light source.

A grainy, microscopic enlargement of a detail from the original 35 mm slide above captures the essence of fishing in the late afternoon.

Derek Doeffinger

Martin Taylor

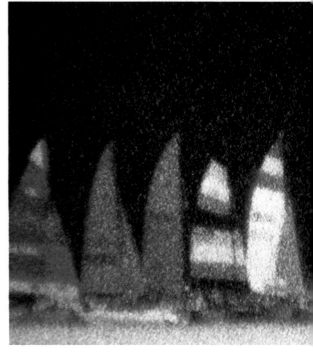

In a photograph that could well be mistaken for a pointillist painting, the brightly colored sailboats are so grainy that they break into specks of distinctly different colors. A portion of the original slide, from Ektachrome 200 film, was magnified nearly fifty times with a microscope.

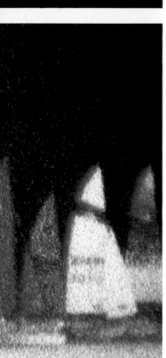

Keith Boas

The Kodacolor 400 negative above shows the entire 135-size frame from which the grainy, intimate close-up at left was made. To get the noticeable grain, a 16-by-20-inch enlargement was first made from the negative. Then a macro lens was used to copy just the face in the enlargement on color slide film.

76

Mixing Film and Light

A characteristic of color slide films that can be deliberately manipulated for a creative effect is color balance. As explained in detail in Part II, the color of light from different sources differs. Sunlight at midday has a relatively even mix of all the visible wavelengths in the spectrum, producing light that is white–without color. Light from incandescent sources, such as spotlights, floodlights, and ordinary household bulbs, contains more wavelengths from the red-yellow end of the spectrum than from the blue-violet end and produces illumination that is more amber in color. Our eyes, however, rarely notice these color differences because our brain tends to accommodate for the color change. A shirt or dress that looked white outside during the day continues to look white inside in the evening, even though the light is actually making it yellowish in hue.

To compensate for this discrepancy between the actual color of light and the way we perceive it, color slide films are adjusted – or balanced – during manufacturing to produce results that look natural to our eyes. Daylight-balanced film is designed to yield authentic-looking colors with sunlight, whereas tungsten-balanced film is extra sensitive to blue to make up for the shortage of blue in incandescent light. Thus, if you use daylight-balanced film with an incandescent light source, your pictures will be very yellow-orange. And if you use tungsten-balanced film in daylight, you will get exaggeratedly blue results.

When deliberately misused, both types of film can dramatically transform the mood of a scene, giving it either an added warmth or coolness. Using daylight-balanced film with an incandescent light usually produces pleasing results because it creates a feeling of warm intimacy. It can be especially effective in conveying the mood of a cozy setting, such as a wood-paneled interior or a small cafe. And as the picture of the young woman at right below shows, it can be used in portraits to create the impression that the source of light was candles or a blazing open hearth. To obtain this fireside effect with daylight-balanced film, simply use a single incandescent light source and position it off to the side at a low angle to the subject. Then underexpose the scene about a half-stop.

Using tungsten-balanced film in sunlight is trickier because an outdoor scene shrouded in blue can look very unnatural. But the effect can be used to add an extra chill to a wintry setting, and as the picture of the lake shows, using tungsten film in daylight is one of the easiest ways to create a scene that looks as if it was photographed under moonlight. Taking a picture by real moonlight with color film is difficult because it requires a long exposure, and because moonlight is reflected sunlight, you will get the same effect as if you had photographed the scene under daylight anyway. The blue cast of tungsten film, together with an underexposure to darken the scene, creates a nighttime effect that actually looks more realistic. The picture should be underexposed by at least two stops. Backlighted scenes work best because foreground objects become dark silhouettes against a rich deep blue sky. If you are using a fully automatic camera, you can deliberately underexpose two stops by temporarily increasing the film-speed setting to four times that of the normal ISO/ASA film rating. If your film has a rating of ISO/ASA 25, for example, set your dial at 100. You can even include the sun in your picture and make it look as though the sun is the moon behind a thin layer of hazy clouds.

Caroline Grimes

One of the best ways to create a scene that appears to be bathed in moonlight is to use tungsten-balanced film in daylight without a filter and to underexpose at least two stops. The technique works especially well with water scenes.

77

Caroline Grimes

Even a subject as cool as a marble statue can be warmed considerably when photographed indoors with no correction filter on daylight-balanced film.

Anthony Boccaccio

In this portrait, the warm glow of firelight was simulated by using daylight-balanced film with a single incandescent light source – a photolamp in an umbrella placed near the floor.

Special Equipment **219**

Infrared Film: In Black and White

Probably the best known of the many special-purpose films available is infrared film. Infrared photography literally extends the vision of the camera beyond the limits of the human eye, providing a new dimension to creative photography. Black-and-white infrared pictures look as though they were taken in an eerie moonlight. A blue sky darkens dramatically; grass, trees, and other vegetation photograph as various tonalities of white, while haze vanishes.

Infrared film is specially designed to be sensitive to the wavelengths that lie just beyond the red end of the visible spectrum; the name means "below red." These wavelengths are basically the same as the wavelengths in visible light except that they are longer and can't be seen.

In black-and-white infrared photography, infrared is recorded as white, just as visible light is recorded as white on regular black-and-white photographs. Images look very different because infrared is reflected and absorbed differently. Healthy green vegetation becomes white because chlorophyl reflects a lot of infrared, whereas the sky darkens because it absorbs most of the infrared. The large water particles in clouds reflect infrared and thus the clouds show up white, but the smaller particles in normal atmospheric haze don't reflect infrared and so the camera usually can see through such haze. Solid particles – smoke and dust – are just as impenetrable as they are for conventional films.

Black-and-white infrared film is also sensitive to two parts of the visible spectrum: the nearby red end of the spectrum and the opposite blue-violet end. To get really striking ultraviolet effects, you must filter out the blue wavelengths. A No. 25 red filter gives the most dramatic results; other red and dark yellow filters produce the effect in varying degrees. If you use infrared film without a filter, the photograph will look much like an ordinary black-and-white picture, but colors will reproduce as somewhat different grey tones. Blues will show up lighter, and reds, greens, and yellows will be darker.

Because infrared wavelengths are longer than visible light, the camera's lens must focus on a plane just behind the one on which it focuses visible light. Many lenses have an infrared index mark on their

Keith Boas

When no filter is used with infrared film, as at left, the tonal rendition of colors is similar to conventional black-and-white film because the infrared film is also sensitive to blue, green, and red wavelengths. With a No. 25 red filter, used below left, the infrared effect is greatly heightened because blue and green wavelengths are blocked, permitting only red and infrared to register on the film.

focusing scale – usually a red line just to the right of the center focusing mark. To use it, simply line up the distance you want with the infrared index mark rather than the center focusing mark. However, to get good depth of field that minimizes the shift in focus, it's always best to use the smallest possible aperture that conditions permit, even if this means using a slow shutter speed and a tripod. If your camera doesn't have an infrared mark, a lens opening of $f/11$ or smaller will usually give good results. If you have to use a larger aperture, try to focus just in front of your subject. With a normal 50 mm lens on a 35 mm camera, for example, a focus setting of 12 feet would be about correct for a subject 15 feet away. If you are shooting without a filter and including both visible and infrared wavelengths, a small aperture is essential.

Getting a good exposure is the trickiest part of using infrared film. To provide acceptable results, the film must be exposed within one stop of correct exposure, a problem that is complicated by the fact that your camera's meter is designed to read visible light waves, not infrared ones. You can use your camera's meter as a rough guide, but it is crucial to bracket by taking additional exposures at one half-stop and one

Recorded on high-speed infrared film, bright sunlight reflecting off these youngsters in a scattering of tones suggests a dreamlike glow.

full stop more and less than the camera indicates. Kodak high-speed infrared film is rated at a film speed of 200, and if you are using a filter and have a meter that reads through the filter, as on most modern cameras, you can simply set this rating on your film-speed dial. If you use a meter that is independent of your camera's optical system, try a rating of 50 to allow for the No. 25 filter.

Unexposed infrared film must be stored under refrigeration at 55° F (13° C) or colder in the original container. Remove it one to two hours before you plan to use it and allow it to reach room temperature while still unopened to prevent moisture from condensing on the film's cold surface. Because of its extreme sensitivity, the film must be handled in total darkness whenever the film magazine is outside the film container. Load and unload the camera in complete darkness, and keep exposed film in its tightly closed film container under refrigeration until it is processed.

In addition to yielding a grainy image, Kodak high-speed infrared film produces a slight halo around bright areas being recorded, adding an abstract quality to the resulting photograph.

78

Infrared Film: In Color

Of all the specialty films, Kodak Ektachrome infrared film produces the most sensational otherworldly effects. The colors are always vivid and usually unnatural looking. And they are not entirely predictable because they are affected by many variables, including the amount of invisible infrared in the scene, the amount of other visible colors that the film is sensitive to, the way infrared is reflected or absorbed by the subject, and the way the visible light and infrared waves, which are recorded on different layers of the film, combine to produce other colors. Also, the filters you use can have a dramatic impact on the final slide.

Ektachrome infrared film was designed originally for aerial surveys – especially of vegetation because diseased or dying plants and trees are recorded in different colors from healthy vegetation. This characteristic not only allows scientists to distinguish between healthy and sick parts of crops or forests, but it also permits the military to spot vegetation-colored paint or cut foliage being used for camouflage. Today the film also has a variety of geological, medical, and other uses.

Like other color films, Ektachrome infrared film has three color-sensitive emulsion layers, but the way that they respond is quite unusual. Two layers are sensitive to the green and red parts of the visible spectrum of light, whereas the other is sensitive to infrared. But the colors the layers reproduce are skewed so that the visible colors are not rendered in the hues we usually see.

The most notable result of this unusual film property is that living vegetation, which reflects a lot of infrared, becomes a purplish red. Medium skin tones tend to become greenish and look almost waxy. A red object that also reflects a lot of infrared will become bright yellow, like the bridge in the picture here.

All the layers on Ektachrome infrared film are also sensitive to blue, and in order to avoid getting an overall dull purplish cast, you must use a filter that absorbs blue light. The recommended filter is a No. 12 yellow filter, but for creative purposes, the effect can be heightened by using the darker No. 15 deep yellow filter. As the series of comparison photos at far right shows, other filters can produce unique results. Filters to try include No. 11 light green, No. 22 orange, No. 25 red, No. 58 green, and No. 81C light amber, as well as some specialty color filters. The picture of the palm trees, for example, was taken with a vivid purple filter.

Because the image on Ektachrome infrared film is formed primarily by the visible light it records, there is no need to adjust the focus as you must with black-and-white infrared film. But it's usually a good idea to use the smallest possible aperture to get the maximum depth of field.

Ektachrome infrared film, rated at a film speed of 200, has a very critical exposure tolerance; it must be exposed within one half-stop of the correct exposure. Because your camera's meter is not designed to read infrared, try additional exposures at one half-stop and one full stop larger and smaller than the one indicated by the camera's meter. If your camera's light sensor is not located behind the filter or if you use a hand-held meter, take your readings at 100 when using a No. 12 or No. 15 filter.

If it is not going to be used immediately, Ektachrome infrared film should be stored in a freezer at 0° to −10° F (−18° to −23° C). Allow six to eight hours for the film to reach room temperature before use, and to prevent condensation from forming on the film, leave the film in its original packing until you are ready to load it in your camera. Load and unload the film in subdued light or, preferably, in complete darkness. The exposed film should be processed immediately in total darkness or stored in a refrigerator.

If you plan to use the film with artificial light, check the instruction sheet for any special filtration or exposure compensation – or in the case of electronic flash, for suggested guide numbers.

Ken Biggs

79

Martin Folb

This delightfully fanciful rendition of Huntington Gardens in Los Angeles was created by exposing Ektachrome infrared film through a No. 15 deep yellow filter.

Doris Barker

A grove of palm trees became a wild science fiction jungle when the false colors of Ektachrome infrared film were further transformed by a Spiratone Vibracolor™ purple filter.

This series shows the effects of using different colored filters with Ektachrome infrared film. The picture at top was taken on conventional Kodachrome 64 film without a filter to show the normal colors of the scene. The three other pictures were taken on Ektachrome infrared film with filters that progressively absorbed more of the blue light in the scene. The second shot was taken with a No. 11 light green filter; the third with a No. 15 deep yellow filter; and the last with a No. 22 orange filter.

Special Equipment **223**

Photomicrography Film

Kodak photomicrography color film 2483 is an extremely fine-grained, high-definition color slide film designed to give a highly sharp image so that scientists and others who photograph through microscopes can take full advantage of the optics in their equipment. In fact, the resolving power of the film – its ability to record fine detail – is far better than the resolving power of most camera lenses.

For the creative photographer, however, the chief reasons for using this special film for pictorial purposes are its high contrast and extraordinarily rich colors. In daylight, 2483 film tends to produce an overall magenta cast. This not only heightens reds, deepens blues, and gives neutral tones a magenta cast, but it also causes greens to become dark and take on a bluer hue. For special effects, this cast is often desirable. But as the comparison pictures at right show, you can get a more natural-looking color balance without forfeiting all of the film's special characteristics by using a green color compensating filter such as a CC20G.

Because of its high contrast, 2483 film can also be used to add contrast to the basically flat lighting on overcast days. But because the film is sensitive to ultraviolet radiation, the slide will take on an overall blue tone. While this blueness can be useful to heighten a rainy scene, a pale amber No. 81A filter will give you a more realistic result and will also eliminate the blue tone the film tends to produce in distant shadows.

Photomicrography film is a very slow-speed film that allows little leeway for improper exposure. The film is rated at ISO/ASA 16, and it's best to bracket by taking additional pictures at one half-stop and one full stop above and below the exposure indicated by your camera's meter. Even in relatively bright light, a tripod may be needed because of the film's slow speed and the light lost through filters.

Photomicrography film should be refrigerated at 55° F (13° C) or colder in the original packaging before it is used. Take it out one to two hours before you plan to use it, and allow it to reach room temperature unopened to prevent condensation from forming on the film's cold surface. The film should be stored refrigerated and processed as soon as possible after exposure.

Keith Boas

This comparison demonstrates the contrast build-up possible with 2483 film. The picture at top shows the normal scene as photographed on Ektachrome 64 film (daylight). The picture above, taken on 2483 film with a CC20G filter, provides much higher contrast, emphasizing colors even in open shade.

Bruce W. Grant

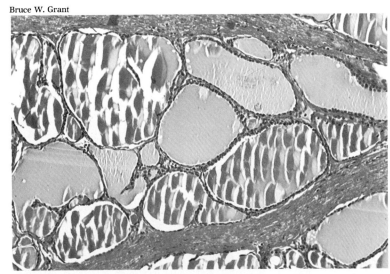

The designed use of 2483 film is to give sharply detailed, enhanced-contrast images of specimens photographed through a microscope, as in this picture of human tissue.

Keith Boas

The sharp triangular lines of the U. S. Air Force Academy's chapel in Boulder, Colorado, are enhanced by the extremely high contrast of photomicrography color film 2483, as well as by its rich blue rendering of the sky. The picture was taken with an ultra-wide-angle 18 mm lens without a filter.

Multiple Exposures: Without Special Equipment

When two or more images are combined to produce another, the results can be extraordinary. One of the easiest ways to combine images is to make a multiple exposure on the same frame of film. You can photograph two different scenes and create a juxtaposition that is visually and thematically related, or you can rephotograph the same scene to create an intriguing illusion.

No special equipment other than a tripod is needed to produce most multiple exposures, although a motor drive accessory can be helpful, as we will see on page 230. If your camera doesn't have a special multiple-exposure button, you can accomplish the same effect by pressing in the rewind button while turning the lever to cock the shutter. To prevent the film from slipping, you will usually also have to turn the rewind knob first to take up the slack in the film magazine, and then hold the knob securely while depressing the rewind button and turning the lever. During time exposures in very dim light, you can also make a multiple exposure by setting the shutter-speed dial on B, locking the shutter open with a cable release, and then placing a lens cap or a piece of black cardboard over the lens between exposures.

When making a multiple exposure in which the images are superimposed on one another, you must reduce each exposure so that the total amount of light reaching the film does not exceed the amount it would receive during a normal exposure; otherwise, the film will be grossly overexposed. The table on page 228 lists the exposure reductions needed for various numbers of exposures. Where depth of field is critical, remember that you can also reduce exposure by increasing the shutter speed rather than by stopping down the aperture. Each shutter speed interval equals one stop. Another way of reducing exposure that is especially useful if you have an automatic camera that can't be switched to manual mode is to change the film-speed setting on your camera. To do this, simply multiply the ISO/ASA rating of your film by the number of exposures you plan to make, and set the resulting number on your film-speed dial. To give yourself as much exposure leeway as possible, it's best to use a slow-speed film when making multiple exposures.

In planning a multiple exposure,

Keith Boas

keep in mind that the relative brightness of areas in the image is very important. White and other bright areas will be recorded at almost their normal value, blocking the other images. On the other hand, black or very dark areas will almost disappear, letting the brighter parts of other images come to the fore.

This lyric tribute to tulips was made by photographing the same scene twice with different filters and using a large lens opening that limited depth of field and allowed the photographer to focus selectively. For the first exposure, a blue filter was used and the camera was focused on the flowers in the rear, blurring the ones in the foreground. For the second exposure, the focus was changed to sharpen the foreground and to allow the background to become blurred. The filter was also changed – to one of vivid magenta.

This illustration of multiple moons was created by panning the camera from left to right while the shutter remained open, pausing at equal intervals for a fraction of a second.

For this powerful composition, a face of a statue was photographed to combine with an image of a graveyard. When mixing very different subjects, it's usually best to keep one image simple and straightforward. It also helps if one image has a dark area upon which the other can show up crisp and bright.

Buildings appear to be mirrored in a street of water in this unusual double exposure. After making the first normal exposure, the photographer turned the camera upside down and reshot the same scene on the same frame of film.

Multiple Exposures

NUMBER OF EXPOSURES	EXPOSURE DECREASE (*F*-STOPS)
2	1
3	$1\frac{1}{3}$
4	2
6	$2\frac{1}{2}$
8	3
16	4

Ken Biggs

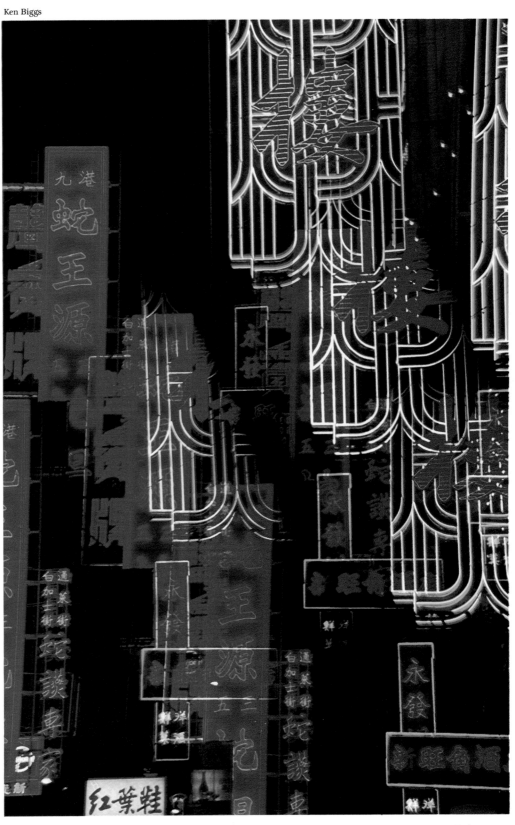

This spirited montage of signs was created by using a multiple-image lens (see page 210) in a multiple exposure. There were two exposures, each of a different scene, with one exposure made through a red filter.

Multiple Exposures: With a Motor Drive

Some standard accessories can help you make unusual and striking multiple exposures in the camera. Most notable among them are the popular automatic film winders, or motor drives, that attach to the bottom of many 35 mm single-lens reflex cameras. The primary purpose of a motor drive is to advance the film and recock the shutter immediately after each exposure so that you are ready to shoot again. Most of them allow you to shoot about two frames per second, although some of the heavier camera/motor-drive combinations can run as high as ten frames per second.

To make a multiple exposure with a motor drive, depress the film rewind button or multiple exposure button to prevent the film from advancing while you move the camera and take a burst of shots with the autowinder. If you pan a moving subject, the result will be a suggestive blur of movement, as in this picture. Or you can shoot a stationary subject with strong vertical or horizontal lines, and the result will be a pattern of staccatolike repetitions. In making a multiple exposure, remember that even a slight amount of camera movement will be greatly exaggerated on film. It is often best to use a tripod with a head that tilts and pans to give you smooth, controlled camera movement.

As when making a regular multiple exposure, you may have to use the rewind knob to take up the slack in your film magazine before shooting. And to prevent the film from slipping, you may have to hold the rewind button while shooting. Exposure for each shot must also be reduced by either setting a higher film speed or using a smaller *f*-stop, as described on page 226. You must use a fairly fast shutter speed – usually 1/60 second or higher – to get the maximum drive rate from your motor-drive unit.

Keith Boas

82

This impressionistic blur of marching drummers is the result of nine exposures in quick succession on the same frame of film. Using a motor drive with a drive rate of three and a half frames per second, the camera was panned to keep the subjects relatively centered. Under a heavily overcast sky, each exposure was 1/125 second at f/16 on Kodacolor II film.

Ghostlike Images

With a simple time-exposure technique, you can turn anyone into an apparition as transparent and ghostly as the ones shown here. You can take two exposures of the same scene and have your subject appear in only one of them. Or you can take several exposures with your subject in different positions.

To make a ghostly time-exposure study, you need dim illumination, slow-speed film, and a very small aperture. You may also need a neutral density filter to cut down on the light reaching the film (see page 202). Mount your camera on a sturdy tripod and set the shutter-speed dial on B. Using a cable release to lock the shutter open, make your first exposure with your model in the scene. Then cover the lens with a dark opaque material, such as black cardboard, and have your model either leave the scene or change positions. Remove the cover to make the next exposure and then close the shutter. Be very careful not to jar the camera when you cover the lens – the reason cardboard is suggested rather than the lens cap. With a relatively long exposure of about 10 seconds or more, you can also have your subject hold still for the first half, then simply walk out of the scene. The ghostlike image will remain, usually without a trace of movement.

As with multiple exposures, your total exposure should be the same as it would be for a normal exposure of the scene. If your calculated exposure is 10 seconds at $f/22$, then you would expose the scene with the subject for 5 seconds and without for 5 seconds. Similarly, as with multiple exposures, the time for each exposure is determined by dividing the normal exposure time by the number of exposures. But as long as the total time is correct, you can make one exposure shorter or longer to give your subject more or less transparency.

Since you will be using a total exposure time far in excess of 1 second, you must increase your initial meter reading of the scene to take into account the reciprocity effect (see page 48). With lengthy exposures, it may be necessary to triple or quadruple the exposure time. Increases can be calculated from the table on page 47. With color film, you may also need to use color compensating filters. If the light in the scene is too dim to give you a reading, take a reading off the white side of an 18 percent grey card or from

Robert Clemens

This ghostly apparition was created by making a double exposure in the dim illumination of an abandoned home. Holding the shutter open with a cable release, the photographer made the first half of the exposure with the model standing in the doorway. He then placed a piece of black cardboard in front of the lens and directed the model to leave the scene. Finally, the photographer uncovered the lens, making the last half of the exposure. Note how the woman's white dress looks almost solid, whereas her darker skin tones permit more of the background to show through.

Alice Sebrell

The picture was made as a series of time exposures, with the subject changing position – and sometimes clothes – between exposures.

Duane Michals

a white piece of paper. Then increase the exposure indicated by two and one-half stops.

The method outlined above is the traditional and generally most useful technique for creating a ghostly transparent image. You can also achieve similar results with an electronic flash. You need a scene that is dark or at least dim enough so that the flash is the main source of light. Calculate a flash-to-subject distance yielding a brightness equal to half the normal flash exposure (or use the guide numbers for the film speed closest to twice the number of your film's ISO/ASA rating). Then with the camera shutter locked open for a time exposure and the subject in position, walk back to the calculated distance and fire the flash, using

the test button. Next have the subject leave the scene and fire the flash from the same distance. Close the shutter. An automatic flash, of course, must be switched to its manual mode to do this.

When making ghostlike images, remember that white or other light-colored clothing will appear less transparent than medium tones such as skin. Black clothing will almost disappear, letting the background predominate.

The undisputed master of the ghostly image is Duane Michals. Here he used the technique of double exposure for an enigmatic portrait of surrealist artist René Magritte, who appears as both a seated apparition and a reflection in the mirror.

83

Trick Scale

When you turn a real three-dimensional world into a flat two-dimensional picture, the viewer needs some way to judge the comparative sizes of the subjects. Most photographers almost instinctively include a visual element that reveals this sense of scale, such as a car in front of a building or trees in a landscape. But by deliberately undermining preconceptions about scale in a photograph, you can create a puzzling and visually striking image. One way to do this, as we saw on page 72, is to move so close to the subject that the viewer has no scale reference. The other approach, illustrated here, is to create an unexpected difference between two subjects of known size.

The easiest way to achieve this effect, known as trick scale, is to make near objects look close to distant ones, as in the picture of a hand apparently holding miniature people. Because of the optical limitations of photography, however, this result is usually difficult to achieve because extremely good depth of field is necessary. To get this degree of sharpness from near to far, use a very wide-angle lens, 28 mm or wider, which has much more depth of field than other lenses. In addition, stop down to the smallest possible aperture, usually $f/16$ or $f/22$, for maximum depth of field. At such a small aperture, you need a bright or fairly bright scene and high-speed film. Of course, you must also line up your near and far subjects carefully to complete the trick effectively.

An apparent difference in scale can also be created when, as in the picture of columns at right, atmospheric haze makes foreground objects appear to be gigantic compared to more distant visual elements.

Cardboard letter stencils, tossed into the air and recorded as they fell, take on the appearance of invaders from outer space.

Tennyson S. K. Huie

Snow obscured the usual points of reference for size in this photograph, making it look as though the couple was taking a stroll amid giant columns.

► *A very wide-angle lens set at its smallest aperture provided such good depth of field that, with the help of a sandbar and shallow tide, the photographer was able to create the illusion of a tiny couple between enormous fingers.*

Robert Llewellyn

84

Panoramas

Nearly all photographers have encountered scenes so expansive that they felt could be recorded only by images of sweeping scope. One way to produce such grand panoramas is with special cameras designed to make a single image on one long strip of film. However, it is possible to make a panoramic print from a picture taken with a 35 mm or roll-film camera. You can compose the picture in the viewfinder, knowing that you will eliminate much of the top and bottom area that you see, or you can carefully apply masking tape to the viewfinder to help you make the composition. After processing, enlarge only the panoramic composition.

Another method for creating a panorama is to take two or more views of a scene with a conventional camera, make prints from them, and then splice the prints together edge to edge. With the camera on a tripod, you can take side-by-side shots by rotating it on the tripod head between exposures. However, if your tripod and camera are not perfectly level for each exposure, the images produced may not match up exactly at the edges. The problem is keystone distortion (see page 82), which is caused by tilting the camera. You must keep the film plane in the camera exactly perpendicular to the horizon at each camera position to avoid keystoning at the edges.

When making a series of panoramic exposures, it helps to use a single-lens reflex camera so that you can look through the lens and line up the exact scenes you are photographing. In sequencing the pictures, look for landmarks – a tree or the edge of a building, for example – to guide you as you divide up the scene. Overlap the shots by a wide margin to avoid any edge distortion caused by the lens and to give yourself leeway in assembling the prints.

Try to keep important elements near the center of the individual photographs so that dividing lines on the final panorama won't be cutting through them. If possible, locate the dividing lines at points that contain large uniform areas of sky, ground, water, sand, or pavement so they will be less noticeable.

Determine exposure from a medium grey tone in the scene or from an 18 percent grey card, and use the same exposure for all pictures in the sequence so that they will have a uniform density. Use negative film if

Norman Kerr

The sweeping scope of a camera especially designed to take panoramas can be seen in this photograph of Chinese dancers performing in their native costumes.

the final images you want are prints. To produce even results, it's also a good idea to send the negatives to a custom photo lab with instructions to give the prints the same exposure. And if you get two sets of identical prints, the extra set can serve as a guide or a backup in case you have difficulty splicing the prints together.

To assemble the prints, trim off the side margins, if any, on one set of prints and join them roughly with pieces of masking tape along the upper and lower edges. Decide where you want the exact breaks to fall and then cut the other set, using a sharp razor knife and a steel ruler. A T square is also helpful. Use dry-mounting tissue and a hot press to mount the prints with their edges butted on a heavy sheet of poster board.

It is possible, though difficult, to include moving subjects in a panorama. This series shows eleven generously overlapping shots that the photographer took in rapid succession as he pivoted his camera 360 degrees. The location is a busy church stairway in Mexico.

85

Keith Boas

This contact strip shows how the photographer planned the shots for a panorama so that they overlap and so that the dividing lines in the final photo fall at the most inconspicuous points.

© 1981 Paul Souza

Photographing TV

Your television set is a unique source of constantly changing images, and it's a fairly simple matter to capture those images on film, either in a straightforward fashion or in a creative style. A tight close-up of a portion of a color television screen can turn subjects into a pointillistic pattern of color. Or you can produce deliberately offbeat colors by manipulating the television set's color controls.

The key to photographing television images successfully is a slow shutter speed. It takes the electronic beam that scans your television screen 1/30 second to form a complete picture, and any shutter speed faster than that won't record an entire image. If you use a rangefinder camera that has a leaf shutter in the lens, you can simply set a shutter speed of 1/30 second or slower to record a television image. But because you will be shooting at close range, where the viewfinder on a rangefinder camera might not show accurately what the lens is recording, it is usually much better to use a single-lens reflex camera. Most SLR cameras have a focal plane shutter – a curtain just in front of the film – that adds a certain complication. The movement of the shutter curtain across the film relative to the movement of the electronic beam across the screen can cause a dark area to appear, as shown in the comparison photographs at far right. To prevent this darkness, you must use a shutter speed of 1/8 second or less. With a slow shutter speed, of course, you should mount your camera on a tripod. And to avoid getting a blurred subject, photograph when there is a temporary pause in the action.

When you photograph, it's best to work in a darkened room to avoid reflections on the television screen. Adjust the contrast of the television picture so that it is slightly lower than normal, and adjust the brightness so that details are clear in both highlighted and shadowed areas. For color shots, use a daylight-balanced film. Because color slide film tends to be extra sensitive to the blue-greens in the television picture, it helps to use a CC40R (red) color compensating filter on the front of your lens. Color negative film doesn't require this correction. Because a television image is relatively dim, use a high-speed ISO/ASA 400 film.

When you take your exposure reading, make sure the television image fills the entire frame on your camera because a surrounding dark area could cause the camera's meter to indicate an overexposure. The meters on some cameras may give an incorrect reading anyway because of the way that the meter responds to the light in the television image. As a rough guide, your aperture should be $f/4$ if you are exposing ISO/ASA 400 color film at 1/30 second, and $f/8$ if you are exposing at 1/8 second. Black-and-white film of the same speed requires about one half-stop less exposure when recording from a color television, and about one and one-half stops less when recording from a black-and-white set's image. It is always best to bracket your exposure by taking additional shots at one stop more and one stop less than the suggested exposure.

This extreme close-up of a color television image reveals the fine points of color that compose it.

In this picture, the color dials on the television were deliberately manipulated to produce bold hues.

Caroline Grimes

These two photographs show the effects different shutter speeds create when a television image is photographed with a focal-plane shutter on a single-lens reflex camera. The picture at left was taken at the recommended 1/8-second shutter speed, whereas the picture below it was taken at 1/125 second, causing a dark band.

One final precaution: many television programs are copyrighted. Taking pictures of a television program might be deemed a violation of the copyright, and responsibility for complying with the copyright requirements must remain with the person taking the photograph.

86

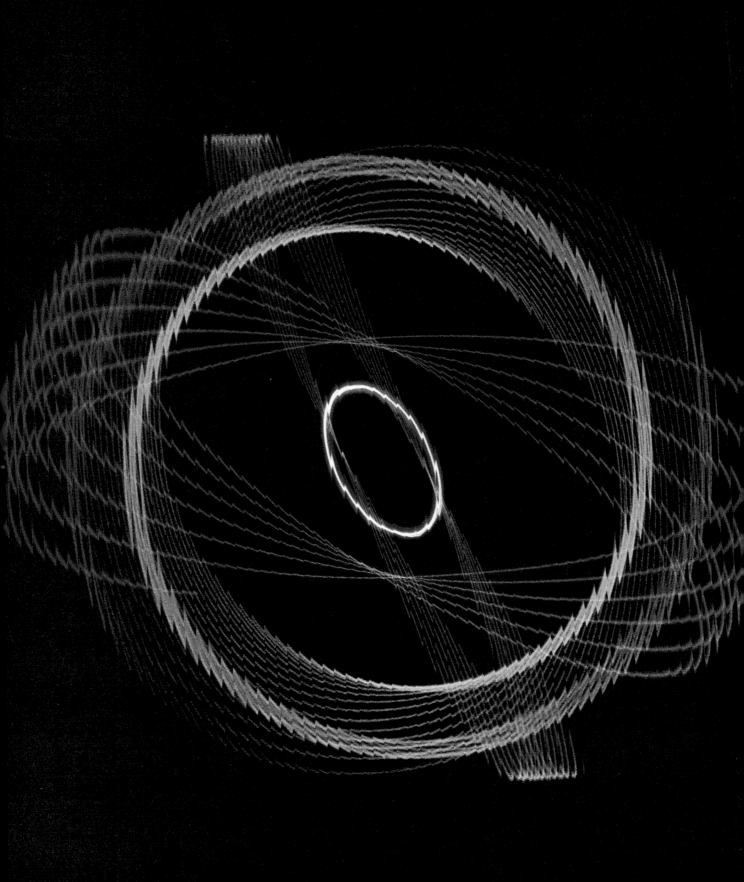

Physiographs

A camera's ability to record patterns that the eye cannot see can be used to produce abstract light designs like the ones shown here. These patterns, or physiographs, are simply the symmetrical light tracings created by a small flashlight swinging like a pendulum on the end of a cord. The camera, set for a time exposure, is placed lens up on the floor directly under the light.

To make physiographs, you need a completely dark room; even a barely discernible amount of light coming in through a crack under a door during a time exposure can ruin the image. For a light source, use either a regular flashlight masked so that it emits only a small point of light or, preferably, a pocket-sized flashlight. Using strong black twine, suspend the light from a ceiling fixture and position it so that it is at an easily reachable height of four or five feet above the camera. With a normal lens, the area viewed at that distance will measure about three feet in width. If you want to capture all of the pendulum's movements, keep them well within that area, or else use a wide-angle lens. You will also need a cable release to control your camera's shutter.

Start the pendulum in motion after turning the flashlight on. Then reach down and open the shutter, using the cable release, being careful to keep your body out of the picture area. Make some tests beforehand to determine the patterns you will get from holding up and releasing the light pendulum from various angles. You can control the light's motion with strings tied to the main one. Remember that the light paths will be brightest and widest when the light is moving slowly and thinnest and faintest when it is moving quickly.

To create light patterns in color, simply put a filter over the camera's lens or the light source. For multiple colors, make a series of time exposures on the same frame of film with different colored filters, leaving the camera's shutter locked open and holding a piece of black cardboard above the lens while you change filters.

You will have to determine the best aperture to use by shooting a test roll. Put your light in motion and record it at every aperture your lens offers. Remember that if you record the light with a filter later, you should increase the exposure by opening the aperture the number of f-stops recommended by the filter manufacturer.

Neil Montanus

Keith Boas

For this stark pattern of cross hatches, a No. 38A blue filter was placed over the lens during the exposure.

With the flashlight pendulum suspended about five feet above the camera, the exposure for this abstract design was f/8 on Kodak Ektachrome 160 film.

Keith Boas

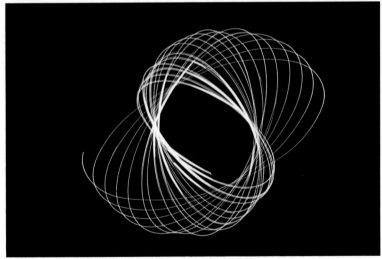

◄ *To create the pleasing multicolored geometric design at left, the photographer made two exposures of a swinging light –one with a magenta filter over the camera lens and the other with a light blue filter. The blue filter allowed the light to be recorded as white in parts of its path.*

87

Crystal Patterns

The vibrantly colored patterns shown here are extreme close-ups of crystals. To take such pictures, scientists usually use elaborate setups that involve a microscope. But many simple chemical compounds produce crystals large enough to be photographed with ordinary close-up equipment.

The source of the brilliant colors is two polarizing screens – one placed between the light source and the slide containing the crystals, and the other placed between the slide and the lens. The polarizer nearest the light source polarizes the light passing through the slide. Wherever a wavelength of polarized light penetrates a crystal, it vibrates in a new direction, often producing a vivid color. The second polarizer, when rotated 90 degrees to the first one, blocks all light from reaching the film except those wavelengths that were modified by the crystal.

Many inexpensive compounds available at your local drugstore can easily be made to crystallize by evaporation. You can also get good crystal formations from most black-and-white photographic developers and fixers sold in powders. To form a crystal subject by evaporation, put a few grains of the dry compound on a clean glass slide and mix them with a couple of drops of water to dissolve them. A 2-by-2-inch glass cover for binding 35 mm slides works fine. Then set the glass aside in a dust-free area to dry for a few hours. If the result appears too thin, repeat the procedure with a clean glass slide, using less water or more chemical. Once you get a crystal formation that looks promising, just put another glass slide over the crystals and slip the sandwich into a metal slide binder.

Other compounds will form crystals only when they are first heated until they melt and are then allowed to cool. Among them are benzoic acid, citric acid, dextrose, and urea. You can melt them with a household iron by sprinkling a few grains of the dry chemicals on a glass slide and applying heat to it from below with a hot iron. To avoid cracking the glass, don't let it touch the iron directly and keep it in constant motion. Hold the slide on the end of a spring clothespin to keep from burning your fingers. Work in a well-ventilated room and be especially careful not to inhale the fumes. When the compound has melted to a liquid, encase it in a tight sandwich by putting a

Allan Horvath

second glass slide on top. Squeeze the two sheets of glass together with spring clothespins. The crystals will form as the sandwich cools.

To photograph crystals, you must be able to obtain high magnifications, so it is best to use a slide copier with a long bellows that lets you get magnifications in the 4x-to-6x range with a macro lens or a reversed regular lens of normal focal length (see page 250). Then you can double or triple this magnification by using other standard close-up devices: auxiliary close-up lenses, extension tubes, or tele-extenders. You can also get greater magnifications by using a macro lens with a long focal length.

To get the sharpest images without the subject jiggling, avoid long exposures by using an electronic flash as your light source. Because of the light lost through extension and the polarizers, the flash should be a fairly powerful unit. Use the diffuser plate on your slide copier to spread the light from the flash, and use a daylight-balanced color slide film for correct color balance with the electronic flash.

This striking pattern of colorful planes was formed by crystals of resorcinol, a compound commonly used as an antiseptic and in the making of dyes. The magnification on the original slide was approximately four times.

Allan Horvath

Crystals, obtained by dissolving a few grains of ordinary Epsom salts in drops of water and then letting the mixture dry, provided this glowing display when photographed through polarizing filters. The crystals were magnified four times on the original slide.

Blacklight Photography

Ultraviolet wavelengths are slightly shorter than those of blue-violet light and are invisible to us. But one visible effect of ultraviolet radiation is its ability to make certain materials fluoresce – to produce light waves that make them seem to glow in the dark. The technique of photographing this phenomenon, known as fluorescent or blacklight photography, is relatively simple and can yield eerie yet beautiful results.

When exposed to a strong ultraviolet source such as the common blacklight fluorescent tube, many everyday objects glow. Among them are some plastic materials and some brightly colored fabrics. Certain cosmetics also fluoresce. And art-supply and craft stores sell fluorescent inks, paints, crayons, and papers that you can apply to objects to make them glow.

Blacklight fluorescent tubes are available in several sizes from hardware and electrical supply stores. The 15-watt size fits easily into a desk lamp or an under-cabinet strip fixture, and two such bulbs will supply enough illumination for most blacklight photography. Whatever size or brand you get, make sure it is marked BLB (blacklight blue). This dark blue tube has a built-in filter that removes virtually all visible light, whereas tubes coded simply BL give off too much white light for blacklight photography. The full code on the 15-watt tubes is F15T8-BLB.

Blacklight pictures should be taken in a completely dark room with the blacklight tubes as the only source of illumination. Since the brightness of fluorescence is relatively weak, position the tubes as close as practical to the subject while maintaining even illumination. Aluminum foil reflectors fitted directly onto the tubes can help you control the brightness and direction of the illumination. Since film is very sensitive to ultraviolet and your intention is to photograph the visible fluorescence, not the ultraviolet itself, you need a filter to absorb the ultraviolet and prevent it from being recorded on film. You can use either a No. 2A or 2B filter – also known as a UV filter.

The dimness of light coming from a fluorescing object is the chief problem in blacklight photography. It is best to use a high-speed daylight-balanced film, such as Kodacolor 400 film for color prints or Kodak Ektachrome 400 film for slides. If you want to accentuate the blues in a scene, use the slightly slower tungsten-balanced Ektachrome 160 film.

Even with fast film, plan on using a tripod and a relatively long exposure time. Also expect to experiment because the meter on most cameras is not sensitive enough to determine accurate exposure for fluorescence. For example, for a group of objects painted with fluorescent paints and illuminated with two 15-watt BLB tubes 12 to 18 inches from the subjects, try a close-up with a 1/4-second exposure time at f/11 on ISO/ASA 400 film. Then bracket on one side with exposures at 1/8, 1/15, 1/30, and 1/60 second and on the other side with ones at 1/2, 1, 2, and 4 seconds.

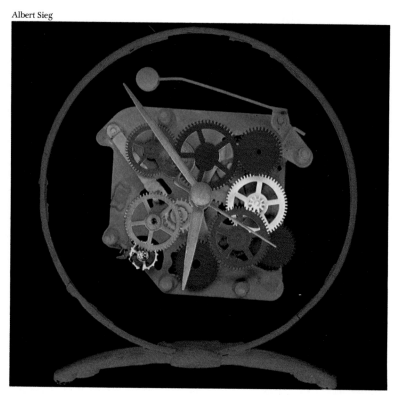

This revealing look at a clock's mechanism was made by disassembling the clockworks and painting the parts with fluorescent paints. It was then reassembled and photographed under a blacklight.

▶

With only ultraviolet, or blacklight, illumination, a wig sprayed with glowing fluorescent paint, combined with fluorescent nail polish and lipstick, created this playful image.

Erich Bach

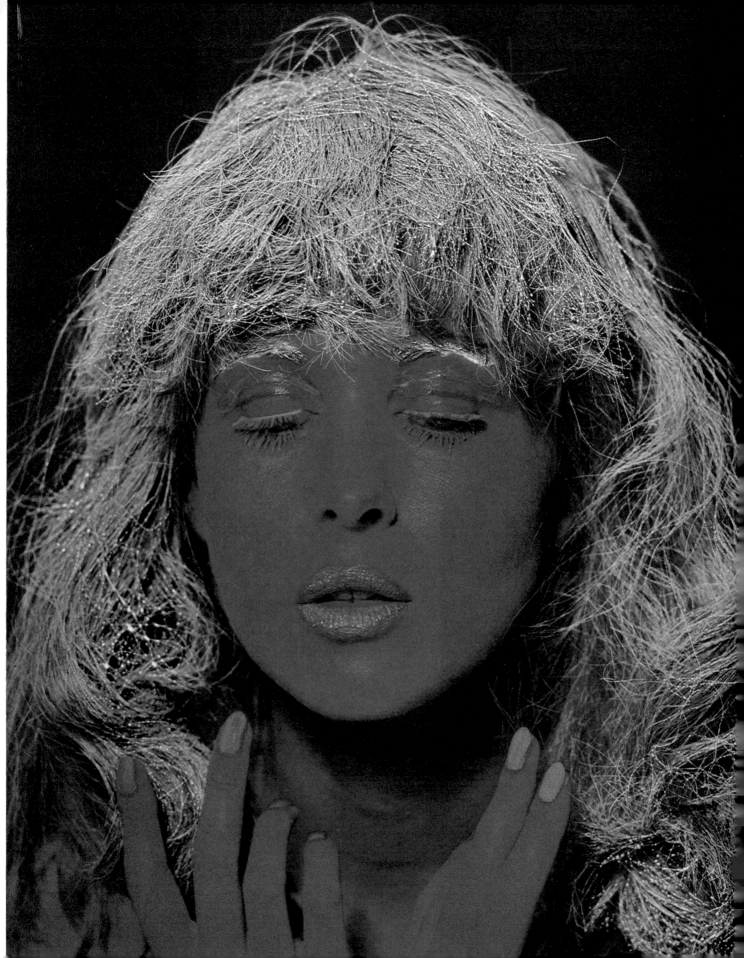

Reverberation

The principle used in pinhole cameras can be reversed to create a projector – a projector that can be used to copy color slides and give them the spectacular impressionistic quality shown in the pictures on these two pages. Basically, light from an intense pinpoint source is projected through the slide and onto the film in a single-lens reflex camera with its lens removed.

The picture produced is an aberration resulting from a pinpoint of light being split into its spectral colors and refracted slightly as it passes through the color slide. In effect, the picture on the slide being copied is turned into several images that do not coincide exactly in size or position, and these mismatches produce a color fringing that makes the final picture look as if it were reverberating.

To carry out the procedure, you need a room that can be darkened totally because even a faint amount of light could ruin the image. For a light source, you should use a high-intensity desk lamp. One with a standard 40-watt high-intensity bulb works well. Punch a tiny hole in a sheet of aluminum foil with a No. 10 sewing needle, following the procedure described on page 246 for pinhole cameras. Center the hole and, making sure that all the edges are completely light-tight, tape the aluminum foil over the front of the lamp. Be sure to leave some air space so that heat produced by the lamp can be dissipated. Even then, turn the lamp on for only brief intervals. The pinhole must be the only source of light in the room. If the lamp leaks light into the room through its ventilation holes, cover them with foil, construction paper, or a cardboard box.

The setup for projecting is simple. Put the lamp on a table, or clamp it to a light stand at one end of the room. Near the other end, arrange the slide and the camera as shown in the diagram at right below. Attach the slide to a light stand or some other support with a clamp or a spring clothespin, and position it so that it is 6 feet (1.8 m) in front of the lamp and in line with it. Place your camera – without its lens – on a tripod, and position it so that it is about 8 inches (20 cm) behind the slide and is in perfect alignment with both the slide and the light source. Then, with the room lights off, turn on the lamp. Look through the viewfinder of

Keith Boas

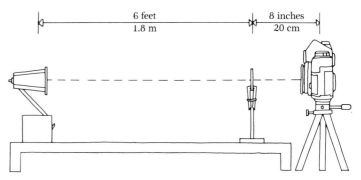

your camera and focus the image by slowly moving the slide back and forth.

For the best color balance, use tungsten-balanced film. Set your camera on B for a time exposure, and equip it with a cable release. In the dark, you can count off the seconds by slowly saying "One thousand one, one thousand two, one thousand three. . . ." Exposure time will vary, depending on the exact pinhole size, lamp wattage, slide density, and distances involved. And your alignment of the slide and camera with the light beam also affects exposure. When you first try your setup, take a test roll, bracketing widely. If you are using a standard 40-watt high-intensity bulb and Kodak Ektachrome 160 film (tungsten) with the distances and pinhole size suggested here, you can try an exposure of 20 seconds as a rough starting point. On subsequent rolls, you should bracket the equivalent of one stop on either side of the testing exposure to allow for variations in slide density. When bracketing time exposures, remember that doubling the time is the equivalent of a one-stop increase, and halving it is the equivalent of a one-stop decrease.

Keith Boas

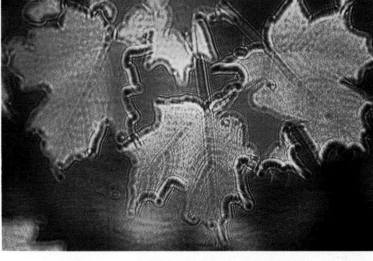

Comparison shots vividly demonstrate the effect of using a pinhole light source to copy a slide. The delicate translucent color of backlighted maple leaves on the original at right was transformed on the copy at top into a vibrant image that conveys the brilliance of autumn foliage.

◄

When picking slides to copy with a pinhole light source, keep in mind the loss of detail that occurs and look for close-ups that have simple subjects and large masses of color.

Even a slide of an ordinary park pigeon was dramatically changed by the visual reverberations occurring when a copy is made with a pinhole light source.

Chuck Fluhr

91

Copying Slides

Slide copying is a technique you can use to alter a slide's color, density, or contrast or to combine two or more images on one transparency. It is basically a form of close-up photography (see page 182). To duplicate a transparency, you need a single-lens reflex camera and an extension device that fits between a lens and the camera body to magnify the subject so that it is the same size or larger on the copying film.

Among the close-up devices you can use for copying slides – at the upper end of the scale both in price and flexibility – are special slide copiers that usually have a bellows and lens mounted on a vertical track over a box. The box contains a built-in electronic flash, diffuser, and filter drawer, and you place the slide on the box to copy. At the other end of the scale, there are simple lens attachments to hold a slide a few inches away from the end of the lens. When used with the proper length of bellows or extension tubes, they produce same-size copies of a slide.

Whatever slide-copying device you use, the final image will be authentically hued only if you use filters to adjust the color balance of the light passing through the original slide. The choice of these will be greatly affected by two factors: the type of film you use and the light source you place behind the slide. An electronic flash, which is attached to the camera in normal fashion with a long cord, is best because it produces illumination consistent in intensity and color balance, and the intensity is usually great enough to let you use a small aperture for greater depth of field.

Since ordinary slide film is designed to produce a sharp, richly colored image when projected on a screen, copies made on it tend to have more contrast and color saturation than the original. To make copy slides of normal contrast, there are two special films: Kodak Ektachrome SE slide duplicating film SO-366 for exposure with electronic flash, and Kodak Ektachrome slide duplicating film 5071 for 3200 K tungsten illumination. Although not intended for slide copying, Kodachrome 25 film gives good results in situations where you don't mind a slight increase in contrast. Since it is a daylight-balanced film, it should be used with an electronic flash.

Keith Boas

To focus attention on the plane and the sunset, the photographer copied the original slide at left using a deep pink split-field filter, which dramatically darkened the expanse of sky below.

To adjust or manipulate the color balance when copying slides, you must create a filter pack of either color compensating or color printing filters and use it along with a UV filter. Determining the exact filter pack you need is usually a matter of trial and error, but it would be helpful to use a guide such as the basic filtration recommendations on the film's instruction sheet or the entry on slide copying in the Kodak book *The Eleventh Here's How.*

Once you have established how to produce a perfect copy of an original, creative effects are the next step. If your equipment permits, you can crop a slide by enlarging a portion of it. You can also copy two or more originals on one slide. And because you can crop the originals, you have more leeway in combining the images than when you simply sandwich slides. To add color to a slide, just slip a filter of the desired color into the filter pack.

Slide copier

Robert Llewellyn

This mysterious image was made by simply combining a slide of the silhouette of a hand and a slide of a star-filled sky.

Robert Llewellyn

92

The textural similarity of a moustache at close range and trees seen from a distance allowed the photographer to create this clever illusion when he copied two original slides onto one transparency. Note how the double exposure is most pronounced where two dark areas overlap.

Copying Projected Images

Another easy way to copy slides is to project your originals onto a screen and photograph them. There are some distinct advantages to copying projections. One is that you can deliberately distort the image by shooting the screen from an unusual angle. And instead of projecting on a screen, you can project the image onto a surface that adds its own texture to the final slide. In addition, if you have access to other projectors, copying projections is one of the easiest ways to create a final image composed of two or more images because you can see exactly how the parts of the picture fit together on the screen.

If you want to project an image onto an unusual surface, look for one that is predominantly light colored, so that most of the light carrying the image will be reflected instead of absorbed. If you want to project the image straightforwardly onto a screen, it is best to use a flat matte white surface instead of a conventional beaded screen to avoid reflected highlights that could make the final image look diffused. The least expensive way to make such a screen is to give a piece of hardboard, such as Masonite, three or four coats of flat white paint.

When shooting projections, it's best to use a single-lens reflex camera so that you can see exactly what the camera is recording. And unless you want to distort the image deliberately, position the camera so that its angle of view coincides as closely as possible with the axis of the projection beam. In an average-sized room, put the camera on a tripod behind the projector, elevated slightly above it, and use a medium telephoto lens. Then crop the image by moving the camera forward or backward. If your projector has a zoom lens, you can also use it to control the size of the image. And the appearance of the final image can be dramatically transformed by placing color filters, diffusers, multiple-image attachments, or vignetting filters in front of either the projector or camera lens.

If you want to combine two or more images, arrange the projectors so that the axes of their projection beams – as well as that of the camera's angle of view – are as close together as possible. The images from projectors placed side by side on a table or one above the other will not usually look noticeably distorted. Choose originals that have large dark areas or that are of low-key subjects to avoid having washed-out bright spots in the overlapping images. You can control brightness on the images by placing neutral density, vignetting, or deep-colored filters in front of the projectors' lenses. Some projectors also have a high/low switch that lets you vary the intensity of the light beam.

For copying projections, you should use tungsten-balanced slide film and work in a darkened room. Determine exposure in the usual manner by taking an overall reading of the projected image with your camera's meter. Depending on the film speed, you will probably have to use a fairly slow shutter speed because of the relative dimness of the projector's light.

Norman Kerr

The ornateness of an Oriental statue was heightened when a slide of the statue was projected onto a piece of brocade.

93

▶
This delightfully puzzling portrait was made by projecting the image of the woman onto a cold, darkened window on which condensation had collected.

Norman Kerr

Pattern Projections

Unusual, eye-catching results can be obtained photographing a scene of a slide projected onto a real subject. As the pictures here demonstrate, the best slides to use are ones showing interesting designs or patterns. And among the most intriguing subjects are nude models because large areas of medium- to light-colored flesh tones will reflect the projected image quite well.

A good source for patterns is a wallpaper sample book. You can flip through it and take close-up slides of patterns you like. Depending on the size of the wallpaper sample you choose, you may need to use a macro lens or a simple screw-in close-up lens on your camera's prime lens. Fabrics and wrapping paper are other sources of patterns. And you can shoot natural patterns such as flower beds, pebbles, leaves, and fence railings. You can also create projectable patterns by sandwiching materials such as lens cleaning tissue, feathers, or loosely woven gauze in a glass slide. And there are special metal slides with stamped patterns that slip directly into your projector and cast a shadow, as in the picture of the young boy here.

You should project the pattern in a darkened room with the projector as the principal or sole source of light. The chief problem you will encounter is keeping the projection from showing up on the background. Whenever possible, position the projector at an oblique angle to the subject so that its projected image doesn't fall on the background. If you want to project directly onto the subject from the front, try a background that is several feet behind the subject. A black background at this distance usually will not reflect enough of the image to be noticeable, and it has the added advantage of dramatically setting off the lighted subject.

The projected image that falls on a light-colored background in the distance can be obscured by lighting the background with one or two photofloods, but you must be careful not to let any of the illumination spill onto your subject and spoil the effect of the pattern. You can also limit the area covered by the projection by cutting a mask out of black cardboard and putting it in front of the projector lens.

Neil Montanus

For color photos, you can use any tungsten-balanced film or a daylight film with a No. 80A or 80B correction filter. You will probably need a high-speed film because of the dimness of the projected image. Even with high-speed film, use a tripod as a compositional aid and convenience because you will be working with your camera and the slide projector simultaneously. Determine your exposure in the usual manner by taking a reading from your camera's meter. But bracket by at least a couple of stops on both sides of the indicated exposure, taking shots at half-stop increments.

When a color slide of an elaborately detailed design on a dark background was projected onto the model, it created a surprisingly rich and mysterious mood.

Neil Montanus

To produce this striking
figure study, a color slide
of a striped wallpaper
pattern was projected
onto the model. A simple,
straightforward pattern
was chosen because it
strongly emphasized
form when distorted by
the body's contours.

Keith Boas

This picture of a young
Halloween trickster was
given a playfully sinister
touch when a metal
pattern slide was
projected on him. The
projector was placed to
one side and angled so
that its image wouldn't
fall on the background.

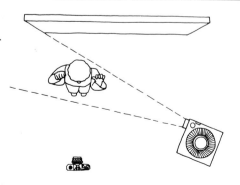

94

Color from Black and White

Many photographers have scores of black-and-white pictures that they would like to include in a slide show. And it is surprisingly easy to make slides from prints, adding a touch of color in the process. All you have to do is rephotograph them on color slide film through a single-color or multicolor filter.

To photograph prints, it's best to use a single-lens reflex camera on a copy stand. If you have a tripod with a reversible center post, it is easy to improvise a copy stand by reversing the post and tilting the tripod head so that the camera points straight downward between the legs of the tripod. Place the print you want to copy under the tripod, and clamp lights in reflectors to two of the tripod legs for illumination. With either the copy stand or the tripod on a table, you will often find it easier to look through the viewfinder if you use a right-angle viewing attachment.

Unless the print you are copying is unusually large, you will need close-up equipment, which also gives you more freedom to crop the image. For top-quality results, it's best to use a macro lens, which has optics specially designed for copying flat subjects. But a supplementary close-up lens or extension tube (see page 182) can also be used with only a minimal loss of sharpness.

In copying, your chief concern should be to give the print even lighting. Position both lights at a 45-degree angle to the print, keeping each at least a foot away. To check that the illumination is even, hold a pencil on end in the center of the platform. Compare the darkness and length of the shadows cast on either side of the pencil, and adjust the lights until the shadows are the same. Two 100-watt photofloods should be sufficient for most copying.

If you are copying a glossy print, you can prevent the camera from being reflected on its surface by making a mask for the camera. To do this, put a sheet of black cardboard in front of the camera, and cut a hole in it just large enough for the lens. You can use a tungsten-balanced slide film, such as Ektachrome 160 film, for copying. If you want a copy print of the original print instead of a slide, simply substitute color negative film. Determine the exposure in the usual manner by taking a meter reading. Bracket at a half-stop above and below the indicated exposure.

Marilyn Unsworth

The stark black-and-white portrait of a young woman above was converted into an intriguing, boldly colored slide at left by copying the print through a Spiralite Vibracolor™ rose filter.

Marc Schiff

A black-and-white print of a snowy street scene was transformed into a cool-toned transparency when the print was photographed on color slide film through a No. 38A blue filter.

Mark Carpenter

A richly hued effect
similar to copper toning
was achieved when the
black-and-white print
above was photographed
on color slide film
through a No. 22
orange filter.

Sandwiching Slides

There are a great many ways that you can use slides to achieve spectacular creative effects. One of the simplest techniques is sandwiching two slides together to create a photographic montage.

When slides are sandwiched, they must be taken out of their cardboard mounts and put into a glass mount. Materials for mounting slides in glass, which can be purchased at photo-supply stores, consist of thin pieces of glass, paper masks, and metal or plastic holders that bind everything together. To remove transparencies from their original cardboard mounts, simply cut each mount close to one of its outer edges with scissors and peel the mount apart, being careful not to cut into the image area of a transparency. To mount the transparencies between glass, first position them in the paper mask, securing each one separately with a tab or a piece of transparent tape along the edge closest to the hinge of the mask. Then put the mask between two pieces of the glass and slip the assembly into a holder. At each stage, clear away any dust on all film and glass surfaces with a camel's hair brush or a can of compressed air, and be careful to handle the film and glass by the edges to prevent fingerprints.

When you select slides to sandwich, keep in mind that the combined density of the two slides should be about the same as one normally exposed slide so that the sandwiched image won't be unusually dark when you project it. Because you can't adjust the relative sizes of the two images to make them merge perfectly, it's usually best for only one of the slides in the sandwich to have a strong subject, with the other one providing supplementary elements. A colorful sunset or a cloud-filled sky with little or no foreground, for example, makes an ideal candidate for the secondary image, as do many straightforward shots of textures and patterns.

You can also produce secondary slides that are soft washes of colors to sandwich with slides lacking color. Simply set your lens on infinity and take an out-of-focus close-up of a solid-colored material such as construction paper or fabric. To produce a light pastel slide, overexpose by about two f-stops. One interesting variation of this technique is to rub the center of the material being copied with white chalk so

Paul Kuzniar

By combining two slides for a new visual interpretation, you can alter the original image's mood and impact.

96

Herb Jones

An unexceptional slide of a boat with a white foggy background was given a highly effective dose of atmosphere when it was sandwiched with a close-up of water droplets on a window.

Herb Jones

You can also sandwich other materials with slides. Here a piece of lens cleaning tissue sandwiched with the slide of a horse gives the image a texture reminiscent of the crackled surface of an old painting. Other good materials are photographic gels, which can alter color or density either dramatically or subtly.

A bleak, almost totally monochromatic slide of a weather-ravaged landscape, below, was redeemed superbly when it was sandwiched with a slide of a golden sunset, bottom.

▼

Keith Boas

that when you take your blurry close-up of it, you'll get a slide with a clear center surrounded by soft color. The slide is ideal for vignetting. The effect is most subtle when you use a fairly neutral-colored material, such as brown or grey construction paper. Another variation is to use a piece of translucent material in place of a secondary slide. Lens cleaning paper, which was used with the slide of the horse, can effectively add texture, and other tissues and transparent materials, such as gels, can alter a slide's color or density.

Special Effects **259**

Contact Sheet Sequences

In addition to putting multiple images on a single frame of film, you can get interesting results by having the images on many frames combine to create a single picture. The most dramatic way of doing this is to shoot a full roll of film so that it shows up on a contact sheet as a unified whole. As the example at right shows, the final picture will be intriguingly fragmented, yet the gridlike pattern of the frames will impart a strong sense of order. You can also cut apart images and rearrange them in an unusual fashion.

A contact sheet is the proof print that is made by placing strips of developed negatives directly on a sheet of photographic paper and exposing them to light to produce positives of the same size. In the case of the size-135 film used in 35 mm cameras, the resulting positives are miniatures measuring only about an inch by an inch and a half each.

When shooting a roll of film for a contact sheet sequence, place your camera on a tripod that has a head that tilts up and down and pans from side to side. First take a series of shots across the top of the scene, going from left to right in sequential increments. Then tilt the camera down a notch and shoot across the scene the same way for the second row. Repeat this procedure until the full roll of film is exposed.

It helps to use a single-lens reflex camera so that you can see exactly what the camera sees. In addition, a moderate to long telephoto lens, at least 135 mm in focal length, is preferable because its limited angle of view lets you divide the scene into controllable fragments.

The key to creating a successful contact sheet sequence lies in planning and experimenting. For your first try, look for a subject, such as a building, that contains some fairly regular elements to use as benchmarks for gauging the position of each image. Then determine the dimensions of the scene by carefully scanning it horizontally and vertically with your camera. While you are doing this, it helps to make marks on the areas surrounding the tripod's panning and tilting axes to note the positions. Next it is a good idea to draw a rough sketch of the scene with a grid so that you can remember the location of the benchmarks. Whenever possible, look for settings that are at a

distance because foreground elements are very difficult to keep aligned.

In determining exposure, take your reading from a middle tone in the scene – or, preferably, from an 18 percent grey card. Use the same exposure for all of the shots so that they have a uniform density. Most custom processing labs produce contact sheets of six rows across regardless of the number of frames in the roll. To get a squared-off image from them, you have to use either a 20-, 24-, or 36-exposure roll. In any event, always have in mind the exact configuration of the final composition when you start planning a contact sheet sequence.

T. Taro

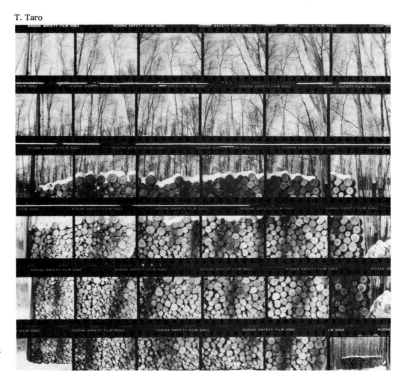

This effective and entertaining contact sheet sequence was photographed with a telephoto lens so that the individual frames, or fragments, would comfortably combine into an overall visual statement. The photographer carefully planned the project – right to the final frame, a view of the entire scene taken with a wide-angle lens.

97

Here's a more carefree approach in which the artist/photographer created an impressionistic portrait of his wife by meticulously selecting and arranging the negative strips.

Roger Pring

Photomosaics

A photomosaic is a variation of the traditional photomontage, but instead of pasting together elements from different photographs, you use copies of the same or similar prints. As these examples show, you can either use repeating copies of an image to create an intriguing pattern, or cut the print into small pieces and reassemble them to produce a fragmented view of the scene.

In making a photomosaic, be sure to start with prints that have the same contrast, tonal intensity, and color balance. With prints of equivalent size and enlargement, this isn't usually a problem. But if you use prints of different sizes, as was done in the boatyard scene here, or if you use prints that show a subject from different angles, as the mosaic of the boy at far right does, it is important to get prints that are as much alike as possible to avoid an unevenness in the final assemblage. It also helps to have spare prints as backups in case you make a mistake.

For cutting prints, you need a sharp razor knife and a metal straightedge. To get precise increments and angles, a T square and a drafting board are helpful. Tack down the print with masking tape to keep it from shifting while you are cutting. If you are cutting the images into a large number of pieces, lightly mark each piece on the back with a key to its placement in the final product, and keep the cut pieces in an orderly arrangement to avoid having a puzzle to put together.

In assembling the mosaic, start by putting the pieces together roughly to determine the exact arrangement you want. If necessary, they can be lightly held in place with tabs of masking tape along the edges. For the final mosaic, adhere the pieces to poster board with photographic mounting cement or mounting tissue. It's usually most practical to start in the center and work outward, trimming off any unevenness along the edges afterwards. Make sure the edges of the pieces are tightly butted against one another, and avoid overlapping pieces whenever possible. If overlapping is necessary, lightly sandpaper the back of the piece so that the raised edge will be less apparent. The completed photomosaic can be treated as the final work, or it can be rephotographed for a more seamless appearance.

Norman Kerr

To create this startlingly fragmented view of a chess table, five identical prints were cut into uniform squares. But pieces from all five prints were used to compose only the table. In the background in particular, few changes were made, giving the overall scene a coherence that heightens the cubistic disintegration of the table.

John Kivlin

An ordinary scene was turned into a series of vibrantly zooming repetitions with prints that consecutively become smaller in size. In a mosaic like this one, mounting the prints one on top of the other would have resulted in too much thickness. It's preferable to cut the prints carefully so that they fit around each other, much like a frame with butted edges.

98

Prints of pictures taken from several different angles were combined in a deliberately loose arrangement to produce this multifaceted mosaic of a teenager.

This elongated version of a cyclist was made by cutting two prints of the same picture into diagonal strips. The strips were cut so that when pieces from the two prints were alternated, each strip contained a portion of the scene on the strip adjacent to it. The strips were staggered, creating a feeling of motion and allowing the photographer to avoid a problem of matching elements.

T. Northmare

Hand Coloring

Before the development of practical color photography in this century, the hand coloring of black-and-white prints was a common practice as an attempt to substitute realistic colors for unnatural greys. The technique has been revived in recent years as a method for transforming a picture, creating images that range from quaintly nostalgic to provocatively modern.

More than most techniques, hand coloring depends on the skill and imagination of the executor, but there are some hints that can help you get started. Most important is the kind of black-and-white print you use. Ideally, the paper should have a matte or semi-matte finish because these surfaces are much easier to work with than a glossy finish. For the colors to show, the image should be fainter than usual and not have too much contrast. When selecting an image, remember that colors won't be evident at all over black or very dark areas.

Before coloring, some photographers prefer to have their prints toned. In toning, the print is placed in a solution that gives a uniform color cast to black and grey areas. This allows the photographer to concentrate on coloring details. White areas in the print are not affected by toning. Sepia toning is perhaps the most familiar, although blue and brown toners are also available.

Whether you tone the print or not, it's best to have a couple of spare prints on hand – one for testing the hue and intensity of the colors and another in case you make an irreversible mistake. For coloring, you can use ordinary watercolors or even food dyes, both of which are water soluble and allow you to rinse away errors. But for the most translucent sharp results, use photographic tinting oils, which are more permanent. All the dyes are available in a large number of colors, and you can obtain any desired shade by mixing or diluting them.

The basic application is the same for all dyes. First secure the print with pieces of masking tape so that it won't accidentally shift. Then, beginning at the top and working down, use cotton balls to dye large areas, cotton swabs to dye the slightly smaller areas, and fine brushes for details. It is best to start with a light shade and build up the color with repeated applications. If they are not widely separated, let one color dry fully before applying the next.

William Paris

Photo tinting oils were meticulously hand applied to selective areas on this print to give the overall image surreal overtones.

Keep a piece of blotting paper handy and put a sheet of paper under your hand as you work to prevent smears. If you want to color only part of a print, it's advisable to cover the area surrounding it with a waterproof material, known as a liquid frisket, which can be applied much like rubber cement and then peeled off afterwards. Both the photo tinting dyes and frisket material are usually stocked at art-supply and photo-specialty dealers.

99

Brooke Hummer

In a scene reminiscent of a turn-of-the-century postcard, straight washes of color were applied consecutively to the sky, water, sand, sidewalk, and foreground. Then the yellow color on the figure's rain cape was carefully applied with a fine brush.

Andrea Crawford

To create this sleek final image, the photographer discriminately added colors to accent the woman's features.

Laser Posterizations

The colors in a photograph normally have tones that range smoothly and continuously from very light through medium tones to very dark. In the process known as posterization, or tone separation, these continuous tones are converted into distinct and separate flat tones. Until recently, the only way this effect could be achieved was through hours of darkroom work. Now, however, a new process using laser technology permits you to obtain posterization effects in an enormous variety of color combinations by sending a 35 mm slide to a special lab.

Much like the electronic beams in color television sets, the LaserColor process uses red, green, and blue laser beams to scan the slide and then reconstruct the image on color negative film. As the laser beam scans the slide, it breaks up the image into millions of tiny dots. These dots are recorded as signals in a computer that processes them, adjusting for the contrast and color balance of the photographic materials being used, as well as for other factors. The computer then guides the laser beam in reconstructing the image on the negative. The entire process takes fewer than 20 seconds, and the resulting color negative is then used to make a color print in conventional fashion.

The main purpose of the LaserColor process is to produce images that match the original slide in color, contrast, and sharpness with more precision than those made by most conventional processes. But through controls on the computer, the process can also use the electrical signals to create several thousand posterized variations of each original. This posterization is called the LaserColor art process.

Not all slides are ideal posterization subjects. Since the process disrupts subtle tonal gradations and eliminates fine details, you should select slides that have distinctive subject forms and uncluttered surroundings. For creating images that are impressionistic in mood, choose low-contrast originals made with flat lighting. Or for a pastel effect, try a slide originally taken with a diffuser on your lens.

LaserColor design previewers are located in about two dozen cities throughout North America, and units are soon to be installed in London and Paris. You can write to the LaserColor laboratory for a list of these locations. Or you can send your slides

Keith Boas

directly to the lab along with a description of the effect you desire – from a subtle art effect to exaggerated posterization. For full details, write to PEC LaserColor Laboratories, P.O. Box 8000, Fairfield Drive, West Palm Beach, Florida 33407.

This series shows only a few of the thousands of posterization effects that can be obtained with the LaserColor art process. The picture at left top shows how the unaltered image on the original slide looked. The middle picture illustrates "true color" posterization, in which the colors in the original were turned into flat tones but not drastically changed in hue. The bottom image illustrates a posterization in which the colors were dramatically transformed.

▶
The flat, two-dimensional effect that posterization produces when it changes continuous tones into distinct, separate tones was enhanced by an original slide with a large area of uniform whiteness.

Michael Newler

This elegant posterization, reminiscent of a nineteenth-century painting in its subject matter and subtle coloring, was created from an original slide that had been taken through a diffusing lens attachment.

Michael Newler

Glossary

Aberration
A characteristic of a lens or mirror that prevents the formation of a perfect image. Aberrations affecting the quality of photographic images produce degraded sharpness, lowered contrast, distorted shape, and color fringing.

Ambient light
The light completely surrounding a subject. Light already existing in an indoor or outdoor setting that is not caused by any illumination supplied by the photographer.

Anamorphic lens
An optical device that has different magnifications horizontally and vertically. Primarily used in the motion picture industry on cameras and projectors for wide-screen presentation.

Aperture
A fixed or adjustable opening in a camera through which light enters to reach the image plane. Aperture size is usually calibrated in f-numbers – the larger the number, the smaller the lens opening.

ASA speed
The emulsion speed (sensitivity) of a film expressed in arithmetic values as determined by the standards of the American National Standards Institute (ANSI). ASA speed values are the same as those obtained by comparable ISO (International Standards Organization) standards (see *ISO speed*).

Automatic camera
A camera with a built-in exposure meter that automatically adjusts the lens opening, shutter speed, or both, for proper exposure.

Backlighting
Illuminating a photographic subject from behind so that the subject stands out vividly against the background, sometimes producing a silhouette effect.

Barrel distortion
A distortion in which straight lines not passing through the center of the image bend outward. The curvature becomes greater along the edges of the frame.

B (bulb) setting
A shutter-speed setting on an adjustable camera that allows for time exposures. When set on B, the shutter will stay open as long as the shutter release button remains depressed.

Bellows
The folding portion (pleated) in view cameras that connects the lens to the camera body. Also a camera accessory that, when inserted between lens and camera body, extends the lens-to-film distance for close focusing.

Blacklight lamps
Readily available lamps that emit ultraviolet radiation, the most common stimulus energy for fluorescent photography.

Bracketing
Taking additional pictures of the subject through a range of exposures when unsure of the correct exposure.

Cable release
A flexible cable extending from a camera that is used to open the camera's shutter by pressing a plunger at the opposite end. The tube, or cable, has a wire inside it and is attached to the camera by means of a threaded fitting.

Color balance
The relative trueness of the colors in color reproduction. Films are balanced to give accurate color rendition in various light sources such as daylight and tungsten light.

Color temperature
A measure expressed in "degrees kelvin" (K) that defines the color of a light source. The color is defined relative to the visual appearance of the light radiated by a special device called a black-body radiator heated to incandescence.

Cross-screen filter
A lens attachment with a grid pattern that scatters the illumination from tiny point sources of light into strong, directional flare patterns. Frequently used in front of a lens to add "star" effects around images of specular highlights and lights.

Daylight film
A reversal color film suitable for use in average daylight (about 5500 K) and with electronic flash and blue flashbulbs.

Definition
The impression of clarity of detail perceived when viewing a photograph.

Defocus
To change the focus of a lens so that the resulting image will be out of focus.

Depth of field
The distance range between the nearest and farthest objects from the camera that appear in sharp focus in a photograph. Generally, depth of field depends on the focal length of the lens, the distance from the lens to the subject, and the lens opening (the smaller the opening, the greater the depth of field).

Exposure
The amount of light allowed to act on a photographic material, which is the product of the illuminance (controlled by the lens opening) and the duration (controlled by shutter speed or enlarging time) of light striking film or paper.

Fast lens
See *Lens speed*.

Flare
Non–image-forming light that strikes the photographic emulsion during exposure. Flare may be caused by light reflected from the lens surface or the interior lens elements; light diffracted off the edges of shutter and aperture blades; or light diffused by scratches, dust, moisture, and so forth, on the lens surface. The effect of flare is to lower the contrast of the image formed.

Flash synchronization
The adjustment and timing of both camera and flash unit so that either the flash fires while the shutter is open or the shutter opens while the flash is firing.

Flat lighting
Lighting that produces a minimum of shadows and very little contrast or modeling on the subject.

Fluorescence
When certain substances are subjected to ultraviolet and shorter wavelengths, they respond by radiating longer wavelengths. If the response occurs only while the stimulus energy is present, it is called *fluorescence*; if it continues after the stimulus is removed, it is called *phosphorescence*.

Focal length
The distance between the film and the optical center of the lens when the lens is focused at infinity. The focal length of the lens of most adjustable cameras is marked in millimetres on the lens mount.

Foreshortening
The apparent compression of depth. The effect becomes more noticeable with lenses of longer focal lengths.

Frontlighting
Light shining on a subject from the direction of the camera.

Gradation
In a picture area, the gradual, continuous change in density or color.

Graininess
The sandlike or granular appearance of a negative, print, or slide. It results from the clumping of silver grains or dye particles during development of the film. Graininess becomes more pronounced with faster films, increased density in a negative, and greater enlargement.

Grey card
A piece of grey cardboard having a neutral grey surface that reflects 18 percent of the light falling on it—approximately the same amount reflected by an average scene. This reflectance is measured with a reflection light meter to determine normal exposure when the subject is inaccessible, reflects too much or too little light for a proper meter reading, or is too small to give a proper reading.

Harris shutter
A shutter containing a strip of three filters with an opaque card at each end to interrupt the flow of light. When used to photograph moving subjects, it produces three exposures (red, green, and blue images) on a single frame of film to create a tri-color effect. Designed and popularized by photographer Robert Harris of Eastman Kodak Company.

High key
In images, ones containing only light and some middle tones, with dark tones completely absent.

Image plane
The plane inside a camera on which a sharp image is formed. It is usually at a right angle to the lens axis.

Infrared film
A film sensitive to infrared radiation, available in both black-and-white and color emulsions. Ideal for experimental pictorial photography when unusual results are desired.

Interchangeable lens
A removable lens for which substitution of lenses of different focal lengths, apertures, or both, is permitted in some cameras.

ISO speed
The emulsion speed (sensitivity) of film as determined by the standards of the International Standards Organization. In these standards, both arithmetic (ASA) and logarithmic (DIN) speed values are expressed in a single ISO term. For example, a film with a speed of ISO 100/21° would have a speed of ASA 100 or 21 DIN.

Kelvin (K)
A temperature scale based on absolute zero as the lowest attainable temperature. The kelvin scale is useful in describing the color of light sources (see *Color Temperature*).

Keystoning
When the image (film) plane is not parallel to the object plane, the shape of an object becomes distorted in the image. In the case of rectilinear objects, the distortion is called *keystoning* because the image shape is a trapezoid, similar to the keystone in an arch.

Lens speed
The largest lens opening (smallest *f*-number) at which a lens can be set. A "fast" lens has a larger opening than a "slow" lens and thereby transmits more light.

Long-focus lens
Refers to a telephoto lens—any lens having a focal length longer than what would be normal for a specific camera.

Low key
In images, those having predominantly dark tones.

Macro lens
A lens that provides continuous focusing from infinity to extreme close-ups, often to a reproduction ratio of 1:2 (half life-size) or 1:1 (life-size).

Modeling light
A lighting arrangement that helps display the three-dimensionality of the subject through variations of light and shadow.

Monochromatic
Of a single color.

Motor drive
A mechanism for advancing the film to the next frame and recocking the shutter, activated by an electric motor usually powered by batteries. Popular for action-sequence photography and for recording images by remote control.

Negative
A negative photographic image. Usually metallic silver or dyes on transparent film.

Normal lens
A lens that makes the image in a photograph appear in perspective similar to what the eye sees. A normal lens has a shorter focal length and a wider field of view than a telephoto lens, and a longer focal length and a narrower field of view than a wide-angle lens.

Open flash
An exposure made by a flash unit during a time exposure (see *Painting with flash*).

Painting with flash
A technique in which a large area can be photographed using only a single flash unit. Achieved by dividing the area into sections, each small enough to be covered by one flash, and then making as many exposures on the film as are required to cover each of these areas.

Panning
Moving a camera to photograph a moving object while keeping the image of the object in the same relative position in the viewfinder.

Parallax
At close distances, the difference between the field of view seen through the viewfinder and that recorded on the film. Parallax is due to the separation between the viewfinder and the lens. There is no parallax with single-lens reflex cameras because the subject is viewed through the picture-taking lens.

Pinhole camera
A camera that has a small hole instead of a lens to admit the light. Although the image produced by a pinhole camera has an overall softness, all objects within the field of view are rendered with an equal degree of sharpness.

Polarizing screen
A filter that transmits light traveling in one plane while absorbing light traveling in other planes. When placed on a camera lens or on light sources, it can eliminate undesirable reflections from a subject such as water, glass, or other objects with shiny surfaces. This filter also darkens blue sky.

Positive
The opposite of a negative. The image on a finished print or transparency, which has the same tonal relationships as those in the original scene.

Prime lens
A standard fixed focal length lens for a given camera.

Push-processing
A technique of intentionally giving extra development to a film to compensate for the loss of contrast that results from underexposing the film.

Reciprocity law
The intensity of the illumination reaching a film multiplied by the exposure time equals the amount of exposure ($E = I \times T$). For example, 1/60 second at $f/11$ is the equivalent exposure to 1/125 second at $f/8$. The law does not hold for very short or very long exposure times, and this *failure* of the law, usually called the reciprocity effect, means that exposure must be increased to obtain normal density, usually at times slower than about 1/4 second and faster than about 1/1000 second.

Reflex camera
A camera in which the scene to be photographed is reflected by mirrors or prisms onto a glass (on top of the camera) for focusing and composition. In a single-lens reflex camera (SLR), the scene is viewed through the same lens that takes the picture, thus avoiding parallax.

Resolving power
Refers to the ability of a lens to image and the ability of a film to record detail. Resolving power is specified in terms of the number of lines per millimetre possible to image and record.

Reversal film
A film that yields a positive image by being reversed from a negative image during processing. Color slide films are reversal films.

Reversal process
Photographic process by which a positive image – as opposed to a negative – is produced on film.

Sandwiching
Binding two or more slides together to create a montage. The sandwich is usually held together by sheets of thin glass for ease in handling and projecting.

Selective focusing
Choosing a lens opening that produces a shallow depth of field. Usually this is done to isolate a subject by causing other elements in the scene to be blurred.

Short-focus lens
Refers to a wide-angle lens - any lens having a focal length shorter than what would be normal for a specific camera.

Shutter
Blades, a curtain, a plate, or some other movable plane in a camera that controls the time during which light reaches the film.

SLR
Refers to a single-lens reflex camera (see *Reflex camera* and *Through-the-lens viewing*).

Soft focus
Effect produced by the use of a special lens attachment to create soft, rather than sharp, outlines where light areas spread into dark areas.

Stopping down
Changing the lens aperture to a smaller opening; for example, from $f/8$ to $f/11$.

Tele-extender
A lens extender placed between the prime (camera) lens and the film plane to lengthen the effective focal length of the prime lens. Also called a teleconverter.

Through-the-lens viewing
Refers to viewing a scene through the same lens through which the light entering the camera will pass. Single-lens reflex cameras feature through-the-lens viewing, which eliminates parallax.

Transparency
A positive photographic image on film, viewed or projected by transmitted light (shining through film).

Tungsten
Metal used in ordinary electric light bulbs or lamps. Tungsten lamps are the most common sources of lighting used in indoor photography.

White light
A mixture of all colors or wavelengths of light. The portion of the visible spectrum comprising approximately equal quantities of red, blue, and green light has the appearance of white light.

Zoom lens
A lens in which the focal length can be adjusted over a wide range.

Bibliography

Adams, Ansel. *Natural Light Photography.*
New York: New York Graphic Society, 1977.

Avon, Dennis, and Hawkins, Andrew.
Photography: A Complete Guide to Technique.
New York: Amphoto Books, 1979.

Blaker, Alfred A. *Photography: Art and Technique.*
San Francisco: W.H. Freeman, 1980.

Callahan, Harry. *Harry Callahan: Color.*
Providence, Rhode Island: Matrix Publications, 1980.

Carroll, John S. *Photographic Lab Handbook.* 5th ed.
Garden City, New York: Amphoto Books, 1979.

Craven, George M.
Object and Image: An Introduction to Photography.
Englewood Cliffs, New Jersey: Prentice-Hall, 1975.

Cole, Stanley. *Amphoto Guide to Basic Photography.*
Garden City, New York: Amphoto Books, 1978.

Curtin, Dennis. *Your Automatic Camera.*
Somerville, Massachusetts: Curtin & London, 1980.

Curtin, Dennis P., and London, Barbara.
What Are You Doing Wrong: With Your Automatic Camera.
Somerville, Massachusetts: Curtin & London, 1980.

Davis, Phil. *Photography.* 3rd ed.
Dubuque, Iowa: William C. Brown Company, 1979.

Editors of Eastman Kodak Company, Rochester, New York:
Adventures in Color-Slide Photography (AE-8). 1975.
Adventures in Existing-Light Photography (AC-44). 1978.
Basic Scientific Photography (N-9). 1977.
Close-Up Photography and Photomacrography (N-12). 1977.
The Fifth and Sixth Here's How (AE-105). 1977.
*Filters and Lens Attachments for Black-and-White
and Color Pictures* (AB-1). 1978.
The Here's How Book of Photography, Volume II. (AE-101).
Seventh through tenth books. 1977.
The Joy of Photography.
Reading, Massachusetts: Addison-Wesley, 1980.
KODAK Films—Color and Black-and-White (AF-1). 1978.
KODAK Guide to 35 mm Photography (AC-95). 1980.
KODAK Master Photoguide (AR-21). 1978.
Planning and Producing Slide Programs (S-30). 1978.
The Third and Fourth Here's How (AE-104). 1975.

Editors of Eastman Kodak Company and editors of Amphoto Books.
Encyclopedia of Practical Photography (AZ-1 through AZ-14).
14 vols. Rochester, New York, and Garden City, New York:
Eastman Kodak Company/Amphoto Books, 1978.

Eisenstaedt, Alfred. *Eisenstaedt's Guide to Photography.*
New York: Viking Press, 1978.

Erwitt, Elliott:
Observations on American Architecture. New York: Viking, 1973.
Photographs and Anti-photographs.
New York: New York Graphic Society, 1972.
The Private Experience. New York: Harper/Crowell, 1974.
Recent Developments. New York: Simon & Schuster, 1978.
Son of Bitch. New York: Viking, 1975.

Freeman, Michael. *The 35 Millimeter Handbook.*
New York: Ziff-Davis, 1980.

Gassan, Arnold. *Handbook for Contemporary Photography.*
Rochester, New York: Light Impressions, 1977.

Goldberg, Vicki, ed.
Photography in Print: Writings from 1916 to the Present.
New York: Simon & Schuster, 1981.

Griel, Tom, and Scanlon, Mark.
Taking Better Pictures with Your 35 mm SLR.
Philadelphia: Lippincott, 1980.

Haas, Ernst:
The Creation. New York: Viking, 1971.
Himalayan Pilgrimage. New York: Viking, 1978.
In America. New York: Viking, 1975.
In Germany. New York: Viking, 1976.

Hedgecoe, John:
The Art of Color Photography. New York: Simon & Schuster, 1978.
The Book of Photography. New York: Alfred A. Knopf, 1976.
John Hedgecoe's Pocket Guide to Practical Photography.
New York: Simon & Schuster, 1979.
The Photographer's Handbook. New York: Alfred A. Knopf, 1977.

Jacobs, Lou, Jr. *Basic Guide to Photography.*
2nd ed. Los Angeles: Petersen Publishing, 1980.

Lahue, Kalton C. *Petersen's Big Book of Photography.*
Los Angeles: Petersen Publishing, 1977.

Langford, Michael:
Better Photography. New York: Focal Press, 1978.
The Step-by-Step Guide to Photography.
New York: Alfred A. Knopf, 1978.

Lathrop, I., and LaCour, M. *Basic Book of Photography.*
Chicago: American Technical, 1979.

London, Barbara. *A Short Course in Photography.*
Somerville, Massachusetts: Curtin & London, 1979.

London, Barbara, and Boyer, Richard:
Photographing Indoors with Your Automatic Camera.
Somerville, Massachusetts: Curtin & London, 1981.
Photographing Outdoors.
Somerville, Massachusetts: Curtin & London, 1981.

Lyons, Nathan, ed. *Photographers on Photography.*
Englewood Cliffs, New Jersey, and Rochester, New York:
Prentice-Hall/The George Eastman House, 1966.

Michals, Duane. *Real Dreams: Photostories by Duane Michals.*
Danbury, New Hampshire: Addison House, 1976.

Michals, Duane, and Cavafy, Constantine. *Homage to Cavafy.*
Danbury, New Hampshire: Addison House, 1978.

Nibbelink, Don D. *Picturing People* (E-99).
Garden City, New York: Amphoto Books, 1976.

Osman, Colin, and Turner, Peter, eds.
Creative Camera Collection.
New York: Coo Press/Two Continents, 1978.

Patterson, Freeman:
Photography and the Art of Seeing.
New York: Van Nostrand Reinhold, 1979.
Photography for the Joy of It.
New York: Van Nostrand Reinhold, 1978.

The Photographers' Gallery, and Bayer, Jonathan.
Reading Photographs: Understanding the Aesthetics of Photography.
New York: Pantheon Books, 1977.

Rehm, Karl M. *Basic Black-and-White Photography.*
Garden City, New York: Amphoto Books, 1976.

Rhode, Robert B., and McCall, Floyd H. *Introduction to Photography.*
3rd ed. New York: Macmillan, 1976.

Rosen, Marvin J.
Introduction to Photography: A Self-Directing Approach.
Boston: Houghton Mifflin, 1976.

Shipman, Carl.
Understanding Photography. Tucson, Arizona: H.P. Books, 1974.
Starting Photography. New York: Focal Press, 1980.

Swedlund, Charles.
Photography: A Handbook of History, Materials, and Processes.
New York: Holt, Rinehart, and Winston, 1974.

Szarkowski, John.
Looking at Photographs: One Hundred Pictures from the Collection of the Museum of Modern Art.
New York: Museum of Modern Art, 1973.

TIME-LIFE Library of Photography, Alexandria, Virginia:
TIME-LIFE, Inc.:
The Art of Photography. 1971.
The Camera. 1970.
Caring for Photographs. 1972.
Color. 1970.
Documentary Photography. 1972.
Frontiers of Photography. 1972.
The Great Photographers. 1971.
The Great Themes. 1970.
Photographing Children. 1971.
Photographing Nature. 1971.
Photography as a Tool. 1970.
Photojournalism. 1971.
Special Problems. 1971.
The Studio. 1971.
Travel Photography. 1972.

Upton, Barbara, and Upton, John. *Photography.*
Boston: Little, Brown and Company, 1976.

White, Minor. *New Zone System Manual.*
Dobbs Ferry, New York: Morgan & Morgan, 1975.

Yulsman, Jerry:
Color Photography Simplified.
Garden City, New York: Amphoto Books, 1977.
The Complete Book of 35 mm Photography.
New York: Coward, McCann, Geoghegan, 1976.

Index

References in *italics* indicate principal discussions